FURTHER
TALKS ON THE

CHURCH LIFE

WATCHMAN NEE

Living Stream Ministry
Anaheim, California • www.lsm.org

Second Edition, August 1997.

ISBN 0-87083-003-1

Published by

Living Stream Ministry
2431 W. La Palma Ave., Anaheim, CA 92801 U.S.A.
P. O. Box 2121, Anaheim, CA 92814 U.S.A.

Printed in the United States of America

99 00 01 02 03 04 / 10 9 8 7 6 5 4 3 2

CONTENTS

PREFACE

This publication is a collection of some further talks on the church life given by Brother Watchman Nee within the period of 1948 through 1951. These talks were given more than ten years after the publication of the messages contained in the book entitled *Concerning Our Missions* (the present title is *The Normal Christian Church Life*). The talk on the unity of the church, printed as chapter four of this book, was given in the year 1951, a short time before his imprisonment, which began in the early part of 1952.

In one of these talks Brother Nee emphasized that the light concerning the church—which the Lord gave him before the year 1937 and which was made known to all his co-workers in 1937 and published in the book *Concerning Our Missions*—cannot be clearer, even after more than ten years' experience and test. In another talk he declared clearly and definitely that he believes all the more in what he had seen before. So these talks are not only an adequate proof that up to the latest part of his ministry Brother Nee still held the same viewpoint as he always did throughout all the time of his ministry concerning the church life, but are also a strong confirmation to the light concerning the practical side of the church life which he received from the Lord and ministered to His Body prior to quite a long time of testing.

Brother Nee's ministry has always been of two sides—the spiritual side and the practical side. Through the publication of some of his books which have been translated into the English language, the spiritual side of his ministry has been made somewhat known and has become a great help to the Lord's people in the English-speaking world. As the Lord's present move in His recovery has spread to the Western World and is prevailingly spreading more and more, we who are some of Brother Nee's co-workers have been deeply burdened to publish several of his books on the practical side of his ministry which can help those who have already been helped by his ministry on the spiritual side to have a full scope and balanced view of the whole ministry committed to him by the Lord for His Body. We fully believe that in the present situation, in which there is much confusion and a number of frustrations and distractions, this will meet the urgent need of so many seeking ones among God's children.

The talk in chapter one on the matter of the church ground is a real remedy to today's perplexity. It affirms that the ground of the church is of two basic things—the authority of the Spirit and the boundary of locality. There is considerable emphasis today on the authority of the Spirit, but almost a complete neglect of the boundary of locality. The matter of locality is even purposely opposed by some and despitefully treated. But it is a test to the proper realization of the practice of the church life.

While the talk in chapter two clarifies the definition of the church in a house (home) and confirms the principle of one locality with only one church, the talk in chapter three shows that a genuine church in any locality must be inclusive. It must have a capacity to include and contain all types of real Christians and all the positive things of the Scriptures; otherwise, it loses the church ground.

The talk in chapter four is very revealing! It points out to us that the genuine unity of the church is the unity of the whole Body of Christ expressed in genuine local churches. All other kinds of unities are unities of divisions.

In summary, the first four chapters tell us clearly, emphatically, and frankly that the denominations are wrong and the churches are local. Any denomination, any sect, any division, is condemned before God. There is no excuse in any case. A church must be local, standing upon the ground of unity, ready to receive all God's children and willing to include all scriptural things.

These talks are the faithful words of one who "kept back nothing that was profitable unto the church" and never "sought to please men." The oppositions he encountered and the persecutions he suffered were mostly due to his faithfulness in his ministry on the practical side of the church life. If he would not "keep back" anything, how can we, his co-workers standing with him in the Lord's interest, keep back anything and not be faithful to the Lord's commission as he has been all the time?

The Lord is sovereign and victorious! He has vindicated His way in the past in the face of the subtle one's opposition and attack. May He increase His vindication continually by bestowing His abundant blessing upon the way ordained by Him for His church and taken by His faithful ones in these last days! He is gracious, trustworthy, and able! He will accomplish what He has spoken. But "he that hath an ear, let him hear what the Spirit saith." "Wisdom is justified by her children."

These messages were originally published in the Chinese language in the spoken form in which they were given. The present English translation, especially the first four chapters, is rendered as literally as possible in order to present most accurately to the readers the author's genuine thought. Attention therefore in translation has been given mostly to the meaning rather than to the language.

Witness Lee

Los Angeles, California, U.S.A.
December 20, 1968

CHAPTER ONE

THE GROUND OF THE CHURCH

(A talk to the brothers and sisters in Shanghai on April 1, 1950, published in *The Open Door,* dated June 30, 1950.)

Question: The brothers and sisters who have been meeting with us for more than ten years all seem to know our ground and how it is different from that of others. The brothers and sisters saved during the past seven or eight years (especially those saved during the most recent six or seven years), however, do not know what our ground is. Therefore, I would like to ask what the actual ground of the church is.

The Importance of This Question

Answer: I think this matter is very important, because the Lord has shown us explicitly in the Bible that the church has a definite ground. I presume we all recognize that the blessing of God, the Holy Spirit of God, the light of God, and even the very life of the Lord Jesus Himself are all in the church. Although we ordinarily stress the Lord's life in individuals, the fact is that His life is in the church. Whether or not a so-called "church" is really the church is very important, because God has committed so many spiritual things to the church. If God had given many spiritual things to us as individuals, the problem would not be so great. But God has shown us in the Bible that He has placed all spiritual things in the church. Therefore, it is a very serious matter whether or not the group of which we are is a church. If we fellowship with many brothers and sisters who are not the church, it will be a great loss.

Let us give an illustration. Some of the sisters who work in hospital laboratories use glass slides for bacterial examinations. For such a purpose, a glass slide is sufficient. However, if a brother or a sister comes to visit, the same kind of glass slide that you use every day cannot be used to serve him a beverage. The glass slide has an important use in the laboratory, but it is useless for serving a brother or a sister a cup of water. The brother is not a grasshopper or a sparrow; he cannot be satisfied with water on a slide. He must be served with a glass. Many problems can never be solved with just a slide. At least you need a glass made up of many slides before you can solve the problem of thirst.

A flat surface can hold much less than a three-dimensional object. We are not seeking to nullify the spiritual attainment of a person before God. An individual may enjoy many spiritual things and sometimes attain great spiritual heights, but God has committed more spiritual things to the church. Therefore, when a person seeks them as an individual, he cannot obtain them. This does not mean that an individual has no blessing, but it does mean that he cannot obtain it by individual seeking. God's riches today are in the church. The church is three-dimensional, just like a drinking glass. As an individual, one must become a part of this "glass" before he can touch the living water. Only the church can contain many spiritual things.

We must clearly see before God that many spiritual things are in the church, not with individuals. The Lord's word, "Upon this rock I will build My church," is very clear and wonderful. The result is that "the gates of Hades shall not prevail against it" (Matt. 16:18). This promise is for the church, not for individuals. Many times it is very difficult for individuals to resist the enemy, but as soon as the church appears, Satan is defeated. In these years we do see individuals experiencing blessings, but their blessings are limited. It is only in the church that the blessings are limitless and rich. Therefore, as soon as a person departs from the way of the church, his blessing is limited and God's presence with him is limited. (I do not say "nonexistent," but I do say "limited.") Furthermore, he is not able to touch many things before God. Please excuse me for speaking very frankly. Especially during the past ten years, I have been watching to see if people know what the church is. Strangely enough, many brothers who have known the Lord for twenty or thirty years do not know God's church. What they have already obtained has gradually declined, and what they think they have cannot be preserved intact. At the same time, there are other brothers and sisters who know God's church. The riches of the Head have become their riches, and they are able to go forward continuously.

Therefore, I wish that all the young brothers and sisters would note that a Christian must be concerned with not only his own gain but also whether or not the brothers and sisters with whom he fellowships are the church. Remember that each person is but an individual. Two may be the church, or they may only be two individuals and not the church. Do not presume that five hundred people gathered together are the church, or a thousand people gathered together are the church. This may not be true. Thank God, one thousand people can become the church, but one thousand people may just be one thousand individuals; thus they are only individuals and still not the church. There is a great difference here. God's children today realize that one person cannot be the church, but they may not acknowledge that one thousand people can be one thousand individuals only and thus still not be the church. Even ten thousand people can remain as ten thousand individuals and not be the church. The church before God has other requirements. Therefore, we as children of God must pay special attention to the ground of the church.

Two Basic Requirements

Today, let me bring out two matters; both must exist before there can be the church. The New Testament clearly shows us two basic requirements: first, the authority of the Holy Spirit; and second, the boundary of locality.

The Authority of the Holy Spirit

We must realize that where there is not the Holy Spirit, there is not the church. The church is absolutely not Witness Lee, Chang Yu-zhi, or Yu Cheng-hwa; the church must only be the Holy Spirit. In other words, the church from beginning to end can only have one authority, one power, and one life, which is the Holy Spirit. There is only one life of the Holy Spirit, only one power of the Holy Spirit, and only one authority of the Holy Spirit. For example, there are many elderly brothers here today. Brother Du may say, "Since I have been in the church for twenty years, I may make a proposal or initiate something." This is something extra coming out as a frustration. When Brother Du is expressed, the Holy Spirit is not here and the church is not here as well. Please remember that wherever the Holy Spirit is not, the church is not. The church is the place through which the Spirit of the Lord may express His desires without any hindrance. As the Lord used the body given to Him by Mary when He was on this earth, so He in the Holy Spirit uses the church today. The church in its highest state is the Body of Christ. In other words, only that which is able to express the mind of the Holy Spirit can be called the church.

Only the Holy Spirit Has Authority

I will go on a little further by speaking first to the elderly brothers. More or less we know what authority is, and we tell the younger brothers to submit to authority. The basic question today is this: When we are obeying authority, whose authority do we obey? Let me say that just as the younger brothers become a disturbance when they speak according to themselves, the elderly ones also become a disturbance when they speak according to themselves. The young ones who speak according to themselves are a disturbance, and the elderly ones who speak according to themselves are also a disturbance. Only the authority of the Holy Spirit is authority. Why then do the younger brothers need to obey the elderly ones? It is because the elderly ones have learned more before God and know more of God's authority; consequently, the Holy Spirit can flow out more easily through them. They are like a water pipe through which water has flowed for years without any blockage. The younger ones should obey the elderly ones, not because the elderly ones are the authority, but because it is easier for the Holy Spirit to speak through the elderly ones. Because they have worked for the Lord for many years, it is easier for the Holy Spirit to flow out of them. We learn to submit to the elder brothers because there is the authority of the Holy Spirit in them. Once I do not obey, I easily lose the authority of the Holy Spirit in me. We are not building up the authority of the elderly brothers, but the authority of the Holy Spirit which easily flows out from the elderly brothers. In other words, the only authority in the church is that of the Holy Spirit. There is no authority that comes out from individuals. The elders do not have authority, the elderly brothers do not have authority, and the spiritual ones also do not have authority. Only the Holy Spirit has authority. This is called the Body of Christ.

An Outlet for the Authority of the Holy Spirit

Recently, I saw what happened to a brother who had carried a very heavy object over a long distance several years ago. His hand felt somewhat sore then, but now it has become so disabled that it can hardly move. The brother said, "My whole body belongs to me except this hand. This member seems to belong to someone else, and it struggles with me." I have never heard anyone say this in such a way before. I am often sick. Through my sickness I found out that whenever the existence of a certain member is felt, that member must certainly have some kind of sickness. When the human body is in perfect condition, there is no consciousness that the body exists. Whenever we feel the lungs breathing, the lungs must be sick. Whenever we feel the heart beating, the heart must be sick. From my birth to my teens, I was never conscious of my teeth, but the day I became conscious of my teeth, I was unable to sleep the whole night. The body is very natural and spontaneous. Its harmony does not result in consciousness of any of its parts; rather, because of its harmony, it does not seem to feel its existence. Today we may not feel like we have fingers. We would regard it as strange to be asked, "Do you feel that you have fingers?" But if one of our fingers is broken, we will feel uncomfortable the whole day. Whenever we feel something, then something is wrong. Whenever the body cannot use one of its members, the body is sick. In order for the Holy Spirit to have complete authority in the church, the whole Body must move freely without any hindrance. As soon as there is hindrance in a certain part, it means the Body is sick. When everyone is under the authority of the Holy Spirit, He can use everyone. Then there is no hindrance in the Body, and everything moves smoothly. When authority operates smoothly, the Body is healthy. When everyone can be used by the Holy Spirit, then the Holy Spirit has authority and everything is very natural and spontaneous. The complete authority of the Holy Spirit is the ground of the church. Where this authority exists, there is the Body of Christ.

A group today may have some brothers and sisters who are under the authority of the Holy Spirit and others who are not under the authority of the Holy Spirit. Immediately, we can see that there is no ground of the church there. The ground of the church is the Holy Spirit. Whenever the Holy Spirit is offended, the ground of the church is lost. The unanimous decision of all the brothers and sisters does not make up the Body of Christ. It is not a matter of sixteen hundred people raising their hands to pass a resolution, and then there is the church. It is not a matter of these sixteen hundred people, but a matter of whether or not the authority of the Holy Spirit has been executed. If the authority of the Holy Spirit is absent, there is no church ground. Only when everyone submits to the authority of the Holy Spirit does the church have its ground.

The body is that which we can freely use and move around in. It has no conflicts or difficulties at all. Whatever we want to do, it does. That which struggles with us is not the body. Whether or not a local church can be manifested depends upon whether or not it can submit to the Holy Spirit. When this kind of submission is manifested, the church is manifested. Therefore, if a brother likes to speak and make decisions by himself, the authority of the Holy Spirit is damaged, the Body of Christ is damaged, and the church is damaged. Consequently, there is no church in that place. A place with a signboard does not constitute a church. Instead, it is only as the brothers and sisters lay down their own thoughts and subject themselves to the authority of the Holy Spirit, allowing the authority of the Holy Spirit to flow through them without any hindrance, that there is the church.

As those who serve God and bear responsibility in the work, we need to remember this one thing: After twenty, thirty, fifty, or even sixty years, when all our hair has become white, we will still be only a transmitter of authority, a channel or mouthpiece of authority. We still will not be the authority. Whenever we become the authority, everything is finished. The brothers and sisters who are workers must thoroughly know what the authority of the Holy Spirit is. Do not think that today we can give some proposals. Our proposals will not do. The Lord has never granted us the authority to make our own proposals. We can only be a channel of authority, not authority itself. If we live to be a hundred years old and have followed the Lord for those hundred years, we should not think that we can give some proposals. Only as our spirit becomes more trained, as we learn something, as the sense of our spirit becomes keener, as we receive more light, and as we touch God's basic principles, thus becoming more familiar with the Word of God, is it easier for the authority of the Holy Spirit to come out through us.

We use authority to serve the brothers and sisters, not to govern them. Authority is just one part of our service. I hope all the leading ones of the home meetings would take note of this. Authority is related to your ministry; it is in fact one of your many ministries. It is not for governing others but for supplying others. In a certain matter other brothers may not see, but we see; they may not understand, but we can understand. Since we understand God's heart's desire, we can tell them of God's desire, saying, "Brothers, you should not do this in such a way; I know this will not do. If you do it, you will violate God's authority. You must give up this matter." This is not exercising authority to govern the brothers, but exercising it with a view to supply and serve them. Before the Lord, we are learning to be an outlet for the Holy Spirit's authority to supply the brothers. We are not governing them. We are learning to let God's authority come out as a supply; we are not here to establish our own authority.

Regardless of what kind of position a brother may have, whether he is an overseer, an apostle, or a deacon, he loses and ruins the ground of the church in its entirety whenever he establishes or manifests his own authority. The ground of the church is entirely established upon the authority of the

Holy Spirit. Whenever His authority is offended, the ground of the church is gone, and problems arise.

When the whole church is under the authority of the Holy Spirit, it is like the Lord's own body given to Him by Mary when He was on this earth. He can speak, listen, and walk as He wishes. The body which Mary prepared for the Lord could not have been more appropriate. His body cooperated with Him to such an extent that it was as if such a body did not exist at all and that the Lord Himself was acting alone. It was so harmonious, so united, so free of problems and conflicts. His hands were never unavailable when they were needed, His eyes never malfunctioned when they were called upon to see, His tongue was never tied when it needed to speak, and His mind was never absent when it needed to think. The church likewise can reach such a level that it is as if it does not exist at all and that Christ is acting alone. The Lord can exercise Himself spontaneously and pass through such an outlet freely. It can be in such harmony, such oneness, and such spontaneity that it is as if the Lord is not passing through it at all. The authority of the Holy Spirit passes through the church so freely and harmoniously that it is as if He has not passed through the church at all. When the authority of the Holy Spirit is able to operate so completely, there is the church. Whenever there is resistance or hindrance, that is not the church. Whenever the Holy Spirit cannot move, whenever individuals stand out, there is some problem and the church is damaged. In such a case, it can no longer be considered the church.

Now I want to go back to today's question. There are many so-called denominational churches. The Lord has not given us the freedom to criticize them. However, we do confess that there are many elderly brothers among us who have come out of the denominations. They know the histories. Many other brothers came out of the world and sin. They do not know how much man's opinions, decisions, methods, organizations, names, and traditions are in the groups that use the name of the Lord. I do not wish to say more about this. From the beginning when we were called out by the Lord, we insisted on a fundamental ground—that is, we must obey and establish the authority of the Holy Spirit in the church and destroy our own authority. I ask the Lord to forgive me for saying this, because the authority of the Holy Spirit does not need to be established by man. Excuse me for using the following illustration for the sake of the younger brothers. If I release a tiger in the streets, is it necessary to send guards to protect it? No, the tiger does not need any guards; it can protect itself. Likewise, the Holy Spirit does not need our support. The authority of the Holy Spirit is in the church. It does not need our zeal to establish it. The only thing needed in God's children is their willingness to consecrate and yield themselves to Him so that the authority of the Holy Spirit can come out of them unceasingly. It is now a matter of whether or not we are willing to consecrate ourselves. Whenever God's children disobey, the authority of the Holy Spirit cannot come out. The basic matter today is whether or not we have consecrated ourselves adequately.

I hope that we will consecrate ourselves afresh to the Lord for the authority of the Holy Spirit. We must pray, "Lord, You are the Head in the church. Grant me the grace that I may not be one who hinders or resists. May I have nothing of my own." We must realize that whenever we bring anything of our own into the church, regardless of how good it is, something extra has been added to the church, and there is a hindrance. My body can only consist of its own members. I cannot allow the things of others to be added to my body. Even the best things of others cannot be put into my body. What is of my body must be my own. The things of others may be precious, but once they are added to my body they may be poisonous. We must learn before God not to bring our own things into the church. Some of them may be very good, but if they are not of the Holy Spirit, they cannot be brought into the church. Once they are in the church, the church loses its ground. In the church there is only one Holy Spirit, one authority, one power, one fellowship, one name. Anything that is brought into the church which is not of the Holy Spirit will ruin the church ground, and then there is no more church.

Anything Not Initiated by the Holy Spirit
Is Not the Church

In Shanghai many people can establish an evangelistic mission, seminary, Bible institute, or Bible study class. Such a mistake is minor. But no one can establish a church! If we are not able to obey the Holy Spirit, and man's authority and man's things come in, there is no church. If it is not started by the Holy Spirit, it is not the church. I do not know whether we have seen the seriousness of this. It is possible for a few of us to establish a factory; this is comparatively easy to do. Allow me to say that we are men who have the leading of the Holy Spirit. Many people in the world who do not have the leading of the Holy Spirit can open a factory. However, the church cannot be started like this. Regardless of whether we are a believer or an unbeliever, whether we have the life of God or not, we cannot establish a church. If it is not started by the Holy Spirit, it is not a church. This is quite a serious matter. No one can start a church, because in the first place, no one has the authority of the Holy Spirit. If there is no authority of the Holy Spirit, there is no church. Regardless of the situation, we cannot establish a church if the Holy Spirit does not start it. First, we must ask, "What about the start?" If the Holy Spirit is not the initiator, we cannot start anything. We must submit ourselves to the mighty power of the Holy Spirit and put ourselves under the authority which operates according to God. We must be wholly restrained and not seek our own freedom. We must let the authority of the Holy Spirit pass through all of us freely.

The Boundary of Locality

In addition to the above, a church has to have a second ground. Without the second element, there also is no ground of the church. We will probably ask: Is it not enough to express and live under the authority of the Holy Spirit? Is this not enough to establish the church? No, it is not. The Bible clearly shows us two things which must exist in order to establish the church: first, the authority of the Holy Spirit, and second, the boundary of locality. If we do not see this, we do not understand the church ground. Does this seem strange? Does this seem like falling ten thousand feet from heaven to earth? Yes, but remember that the church is also on earth. It is part heavenly and part earthly. The heavenly part concerns the authority of the Holy Spirit; the earthly part concerns the boundary of locality. This is a very wonderful matter in the Bible. The Bible clearly shows us this one thing: The church absolutely belongs to a locality, such as the church in Jerusalem (Acts 8:1), which is a place; the church in Corinth (1 Cor. 1:2), which is a place; the church in Antioch (Acts 13:1), which is a city; and the church in Ephesus (Rev. 2:1), which is a seaport. In the Bible the ground of the church is the locality where the church is. The churches all take locality as the boundary.

Here is a special point; please pay attention to it. If the brothers and sisters in Shanghai desire to stand on the church ground, they can only stand on the ground of the Holy Spirit and the ground of Shanghai. They must stand on the ground of the Holy Spirit and also on the ground of Shanghai because Shanghai is the locality in which they live. Once we disregard locality, we immediately lose the ground of the church. Let me give a few illustrations.

The Church and the Churches

Acts 9:31 speaks of the churches in Judea. The church spoken of here is plural in Greek, English, and Chinese. It is the churches in Judea. It is plural in number because at that time Judea was a province of Rome. Since a province included many localities, there were many churches. Thus, the Bible does not speak of the church in Judea, but the churches in Judea. In the Scriptures there is only a local church, not a provincial church. The same is true of Galatia, which was a province consisting of many localities; therefore, Galatians 1:2 says, "The churches of Galatia." Ephesus is a seaport, a locality; therefore, the church in Ephesus is referred to in the singular. This point is very clear in the Bible. Philadelphia was a city, and only one church existed there. Asia, which is Asia Minor today, was a large province; therefore, the Bible says, "The seven churches which are in Asia," not the church which is in Asia (Rev. 1:4).

Only One Church in One Locality

There is one thing we must all notice: The world does not have a church; therefore, the Roman Catholic Church is wrong. A country does not have a church; therefore, the Anglican Church (i.e., the Church of England or the Episcopal Church) is wrong. A province does not have a church, nor does a race. In the Bible only the smallest administrative unit is related to the church—only a locality or a city has a church. The church in one locality cannot combine with the church in another locality to become one church. Each city can only be matched with one church, just as a husband can only be matched with one wife. Therefore, in Antioch, there is the church in Antioch, not the churches in Antioch. It would be wrong to say the churches in Antioch. According to God's arrangement, a locality can only be matched with one church, not many churches. In the Bible we can never find *the churches in Corinth* or *the churches in Antioch*. But the Bible does say *the church in Antioch, the church in Philippi,* and *the church in Philadelphia*. All of these churches are referred to in the singular. There were not multiple churches in Antioch, Philippi, or Philadelphia.

God's arrangement for the church on the spiritual side is the authority of the Holy Spirit, and in its outward appearance, it is the limitation of locality. When the church in Corinth was about to divide itself into four parts, Paul immediately rebuked them for being divisive and fleshy (1 Cor. 1:10-13; 3:3-4). When the Corinthians were about to divide into a few smaller churches, one of Paul, another of Cephas, another of Apollos, and another of Christ, the Holy Spirit said that was fleshy. Each city, each locality, can only be matched with one church. Whenever more than one appears, it is a division, a sect, which God rejects. From God's point of view, the church in Corinth became fleshy because there can only be one church in one locality; a second church can never be established. If one church is already established, the second is a division and is fleshy. There can never be more than one church in one locality. Someone may say that he desires to supply others with spiritual food, but supplying spiritual food is not sufficient ground to establish a church. Someone may say that he wants to help others to understand the Bible, but helping others understand the Bible is also not sufficient ground to establish a church. Neither is teaching others to know the Holy Spirit adequate grounds for establishing a church. Someone may say that we need a revival and that a revival church should be established. Recently in a certain place, someone established a Revival Church for the sole purpose of revival, but revival is not sufficient grounds to establish a church. Men cannot establish a church, because men do not have the ground to establish a church. Paul did not have the ground to establish a church; neither did Cephas or Apollos. Ephesus had the ground to establish a church, but Paul was not equal to Ephesus. Corinth had the ground to establish a church, but Paul was not equal to Corinth. Neither was Cephas or Apollos; they were all not equal to Corinth. They did not have the ground, and they were not qualified to establish a church, because a church must be matched with a locality. Anything that comes short of a locality cannot establish a church. If there is no locality, there is no church. It is more than evident that God takes the boundary of locality as the ground.

There Can Only Be One Church in Shanghai

In Shanghai the church does not stand on denominationalism, sectarianism, or any other ground, but on the ground of Shanghai. This is the church in Shanghai. Suppose I have a quarrel with Brother Chang. I let him meet on Nanyang Road, while I find a place on North Szechuan Road. One goes south and the other goes north in the opposite direction. At North Szechuan Road I can preach the gospel, and a group of people can be saved. While the meeting hall on Nanyang Road can seat 2,400 people, I can build a bigger hall to seat 2,600. Even though I preach the gospel and start a meeting, bringing many to salvation, giving messages, and edifying the saints, I can never become the church because the qualification to take Shanghai as the ground of the church has already been taken. I am not qualified to set up another church because there can only be one church in Shanghai.

A Church Can Only Be Established in a Locality Where No Church Exists

Today in Bijie in Kweichow province, no one has taken the standing of establishing a church on the ground of locality. If anyone desires to establish a church, it is all right for him to go to Bijie because in one locality there can only be one local church. If an additional church appears there, God will say that is a division. It is just like a woman matching a man. If a man does not have a wife yet, she can marry him and be his wife. If he already has a wife, how can she become his mate? She can only be the mate of a man who has no wife. The whole New Testament tells us this one thing: The church is local. We must see that the church is local. The Epistles speak of the church in Corinth and the church in Ephesus. Revelation speaks of the *seven* churches in Asia. In each locality there is only one church. The church cannot become independent of locality.

Please remember that a church can only be established in a locality where there is no church. If there is a church in a certain locality, we can only join it; we cannot set up another one. Once we set up another one, that is a division, a sect, which is condemned by God. I want to ask, "What is the difference between a woman who is a man's wife and a concubine?" Everything is the same, except the position. Only the ground is different; everything else is the same. Though outwardly they may appear alike, something is lacking in one— the ground.

What Is Division?

What is division? Division is to be without the ground, and to be without the ground is to be divisive, and is something condemned by God. Please forgive me for using Bijie as an example again. What is the difference between going to Bijie to preach the gospel, to save people, and to edify saints and going to North Szechuan Road in Shanghai to do the same thing? Outwardly, there is no difference. It is not that people cannot be saved and receive eternal life when the gospel is preached at North Szechuan Road; neither is it that the people at North Szechuan Road will lose their experience of salvation. The gospel truth is the same, and the messages may be the same. Everything seems to be the same. But we cannot establish another church at North Szechuan Road. If we go to North Szechuan Road to establish a church, that is a division. The messages given in Bijie may be exactly the same as the messages given at North Szechuan Road, but in the two different localities there are two different grounds. In Bijie it may be the church, while at North Szechuan Road it is a division. The same message is given at these two localities, but what a difference there is! Suppose we set up the Lord's table in Bijie, that is, the Lord's supper, the breaking of bread. If we move the table with all the attendants from Bijie to North Szechuan Road, we may pray in the same manner as before, study the Bible as before, and praise the Lord as before. In these things there is no difference at all, but in Bijie there is a church, while there is a division at North Szechuan Road. When a woman marries a single man, she is his wife; if she marries a man who is already married, she is not his wife. When we go to a place where there is no church, we can establish one. But in a place where there is already a church, we can only join it, we cannot set up another one. This is a basic principle in the Bible. If we do not care for the boundary of locality, everything is finished. If we discard this basic ground, we have no ground.

I hope that before God we understand these two points: First, God's church is established upon the authority of the Holy Spirit; second, God's church is established with the boundary of locality. The ground of the church is something according to the guidance of the Holy Spirit. We cannot say, "The Holy Spirit has guided us to meet at North Szechuan Road." In regard to the guidance of the Holy Spirit, the first thing He would argue is that the place where we are meeting is wrong. Consequently, we violate and offend the first limitation of the Holy Spirit, and we have no ground on which to stand. Saying that we have the Holy Spirit is not enough; we must also pay attention to the boundary of locality, which is set up by the Holy Spirit. We can never violate the boundary of locality; we can only submit. Men have no freedom in the jurisdiction of locality set up by the Holy Spirit.

Locality Restricting the Formation of Divisions

I hope the brothers and sisters will hold fast to this basic principle. If they do, they will be clear about the standing of the so-called denominations, churches, groups, and organizations. If any group is not built upon the ground of locality, we can see that it is not the church. Are we clear? Is this not amazing? I am amazed when I read this in the Word. Going from the authority of the Holy Spirit to the boundary of locality seems like dropping ten thousand feet from the heavens all the way down to the earth. The Bible reveals that the ground of the church is based on the authority of the Holy Spirit. However, the Bible also shows us that just having the Holy Spirit is not enough; we also need the match of the ground of locality. These two together produce the church. As we look back, things become clearer and clearer, and more and more we have to praise the Lord. In the past two thousand years, if the people in the church had been willing to be limited by locality, there would not have been the difficulties and confusion. If man had submitted to God's authority, neither Catholicism nor Protestantism could ever have been established. Neither could the more than one hundred denominations in China and more than six hundred major organizations and five thousand minor organizations in the world today have been established. All would have been restricted by the boundary of locality.

Locality Never Being Subject to Change

Excuse me for using political terms. A dynasty may change, but a locality never changes; a political party may change, but not a locality; a country may even change, but a locality does not. Shanghai has always remained Shanghai, and Ch'ang-ch'un has always remained Ch'ang-ch'un. During the Ching Dynasty, Shanghai was Shanghai; during the Republic, Shanghai was still Shanghai; even now Shanghai remains Shanghai. During the Sino-Japanese War when the country almost became part of another country, the locality remained the same. Many things will change, but the locality will never change. God wills the locality as the ground for the church. We have the church in Rome as a locality, but never the church of the Roman Empire. The name is similar, but in fact they are different. The church in the city of Rome is recognized by the Holy Spirit, but not the church of the Roman Empire. For this reason, we must learn before God to keep the ground of locality.

Please remember this one thing: The church must stand on the ground of locality. For many years we have been standing on this ground, rejecting all that is not in keeping with this ground, rejecting all other labels. Any group which does not take the locality as its ground is not the church. The service we have entered into here is with the hope of building up the church in Shanghai. If an inquiry is made about this matter by an outsider, we must make it clear to him that the church has the authority of the Holy Spirit inwardly as the content and the boundary of locality outwardly. The authority of the Holy Spirit plus the boundary of locality make the church. If there is no authority of the Holy Spirit within and no boundary of locality without, there is not the church.

The Church Ground and Spiritual Blessing

The clearer the ground of the church is, the richer are the spiritual blessings. In these recent years and in particular during the past one or two years, we have seen God blessing the church ground. Many brothers and sisters have begun to see the difference between the way of individualism and the ground of the church. As the authority of the Holy Spirit is manifested in all the members, causing them to serve God in coordination rather than in individual activities, we see the Lord's blessing. In some local churches the members increase twofold, fivefold, and tenfold—all in multiples.

Originally there were only thirty or more members in Taipei, but now they have increased to over a thousand. We have sent some brothers there, and they have worked very diligently. God has continued to bless, and the members have continued to increase. When I was in Hong Kong, I received a letter from a brother. I feel this brother knows what the church is because of the following incident. The church in Taipei expected Brother Witness to be responsible for their gospel campaign during the Chinese New Year. After this decision was reached, Brother Witness had to come to see me in Hong Kong concerning some matters. They were really disappointed because they thought that they could not carry out the campaign themselves. Brother Witness said to them, "To have Witness is just to have one more brother; to lose Witness is just to lose one brother." If there is a church in Taipei, having or losing Brother Witness is just a matter of having or losing one brother. However, if there were no church in Taipei, it would be terrible. In the end, the brothers in Taipei preached the gospel. Some of the brothers who you would think could not preach the gospel preached the gospel contrary to expectation. As a result, over fourteen hundred people received the Lord. At the follow-up meetings, two hundred twenty-eight people were baptized on the first day alone. It does not matter whether a brother is taken away or added, because there is still the church. Now I will come back to that brother's letter. I am very pleased with his statement: "I believe that if the brothers learn to serve the Lord in a coordinated way, whether there are three thousand or ten thousand newly saved ones, we will be able to absorb them. When the church comes into being and begins to function, it can absorb five hundred new believers if five hundred come, and one thousand if one thousand come." What is this? This is God's church.

A Vessel Needed to Contain God's Blessing

Some of us pray that the Lord would bless us as He blessed the church during Pentecost. But if the Lord really answered our prayers, what would we do? If the Lord really granted us the blessing of Pentecost, what would we do? If the Lord gave us three thousand or five thousand people, what would we do? If several thousand people suddenly filled our meeting place, we would immediately see that we would not be able to absorb them all. If three thousand people were added in Shanghai at one time, we could not absorb them. We would not know how to baptize them, how to divide them into different home meetings for the Lord's table, how to edify them, and how to visit them. However, when God blesses and the church is strong, we can easily absorb them. Regardless of how many come, we will not drag along through our inability to handle them adequately. We now have about fifteen to sixteen hundred brothers and sisters among us; our fellowship is not adequately covered already. What would we do if another thousand were added? It would be hard for us to bear them if God should bless us with that many. We are not talking about an organization but a container that can bear God's blessing. If God blessed us by giving us three thousand and then two thousand disappeared after two days, this would not be the church. If we do not know when people come and when people go, or how many have been added or how many have been lost, this is not the church. The church is a container of such capacity that it is able to contain God's blessing. A church is supposed to attain to such a degree that when God blesses—abundantly blesses—there is a vessel which is able to contain this blessing.

When all the brothers and sisters obey the Holy Spirit, they will all rise up to serve and receive the blessing. No one will bring in his own opinions, but everyone will be occupied with service. When this happens, God's church will come forth. If we are not getting ready for the Holy Spirit's work, He will not work. We must be prepared for the Holy Spirit's work. We must always prepare more room. We would rather let the Lord bring people in than let Him take people out. When the Holy Spirit begins to work, we will really see that there is not enough room. We must prepare for the Holy Spirit's work. We must prepare a larger meeting place and enlarge our capacity; then the Lord will bless. We must prepare men for service; then the Lord will bless. If we do not prepare everyone for service, the Holy Spirit will have no way to work.

All Must Learn to Serve

I hope the brothers and sisters will see that the ground of the church is based on locality and on the authority of the

Holy Spirit. For the authority of the Holy Spirit to come in means that every person learns to reject his own ideas and submit to God's authority. As everyone learns to serve, the church of God appears. As the church, it is not sufficient that our own personal opinions are denied. On the positive side, everyone must submit to the authority of the Holy Spirit. Once we submit to the authority of the Holy Spirit, the Holy Spirit immediately will direct and instruct everyone to serve.

I would ask the leading brothers, especially the leading ones in the home meetings, to excuse me for saying the following words: The minimum responsibility you have before God is to serve, but this is not enough. If you can only serve but cannot bring others into service, you have failed. The Holy Spirit is directing every person to serve. On the negative side, do not bring in your own ideas; on the positive side, let the Holy Spirit direct everyone to serve. The authority of the Holy Spirit means that the Holy Spirit can pass through everyone, the Holy Spirit can direct everyone.

Therefore, whoever can only serve by himself, but cannot commit things to others, is a failure. Whoever does not hold responsibility in his own hands, but distributes it to the brothers and sisters that they may share in the same work, is useful in God's hand. We should not think that we must do everything when situations arise. Those who hurriedly finish things themselves, who hold things in their hands, and who will not assign them to others are hindering the work of the Holy Spirit. Responsibilities must be distributed; they should not be retained in our own hands. Retaining things in our own hands is a hindrance. Things should not get stuck to us. When the authority of the Holy Spirit is given full freedom in the church, it no longer is a matter of doing it or not, but it is a matter of letting the Holy Spirit have the freedom to release Himself. When the authority of the Holy Spirit works, moves, and is released in the whole Body, that is the church. The work must always be distributed. Distribution is a principle. Whenever a responsibility comes upon us, we should distribute it immediately. A thing may be done by one person, or it may be done by five persons. It is better, however, to distribute it among five persons. Always be involved and always involve others. If we practice this, we are training the brothers and providing them the proper guidance. In this way, everyone will learn to serve.

Brother Witness Lee and I have had a long time of looking to the Lord and conversing. We believe all the more in what we have seen before. In the days ahead God will certainly take the way of migration. Therefore, every brother must be trained. We should not hope that people will migrate to Nanchang in the future, yet expect the church in Nanchang to train them for us. We have to train them now. I am afraid that the brothers and sisters have no training before God, and when the time of migration arrives, such ones will not be able to go out. Therefore, everyone must learn something concerning the church. We must learn much more before God regarding how the whole Body serves. If we do this, there will be a way for God to go out from us.

A message by Watchman Nee, recorded by Brother Kun-min and others.

April 1, 1950

CHAPTER TWO

THE CHURCH IN THE CITY
AND THE CHURCH IN THE HOUSE

(A talk to the brothers and sisters in Shanghai on April 1, 1950, published in *The Open Door,* dated June 30, 1950.)

Question: Concerning the ground of the church, we have said that there should be only one church in a city, because there is only one unit. Some people, however, speak of "the church in a house," quoting the Scriptures as their basis, as being an additional unit to the locality. They imply that the church may possibly have several units in a locality. What should we say to this kind of statement?

Answer: The New Testament has a total of four passages which refer to "the church in a house," that is, in a home.

Romans 16:5

"And greet the church, which is in their house." "Their" refers to Prisca and Aquila mentioned in verse 3. Here the fact is simple. The church in Rome, like hundreds and thousands of other local churches, first started in the house of a brother. This means that the principal members of such a house were brothers and sisters in the Lord. At the same time, there were not many members in the church; therefore, they used this brother's house for their meeting place. This is a historical matter, not a doctrinal matter. It is possible to give an explanation for a doctrine, but it is impossible to give an explanation for historical events, because historical events are facts. Anyone who is acquainted with history knows that hundreds and thousands of churches first started in homes. Therefore, the church in a certain place became the church in a certain person's house. The church in Rome was the church in Prisca and Aquila's home.

Question: Some say that since Paul sent greetings to the church in Rome as well as to the church in a house, this signifies that there was not only a local church but also a church in a house. Are there not, therefore, two churches?

Answer: Let us consider the matter slowly. I fear that you have not listened to the word of God carefully. The book of Romans never speaks of "the church in Rome." How then could the apostle have greeted the church in Rome? The book of Romans does not present clearly in writing one greeting to "the church in Rome" and another greeting to "the church in the house." But in greeting the church in the house of Prisca and Aquila, it is implied that such a greeting is to the church in Rome, which was meeting in Prisca and Aquila's house. Hence, the church in Rome was the church in Prisca and Aquila's house.

I presume the difficulty of those who argue about the church in both the house and the locality lies in the fact that after verse 5 Paul mentions so many names. I think all Bible expositors know that after Paul greeted the church in verse 5, he purposely mentioned several important *individuals* and especially greeted them one by one. This does not mean, however, that these people were *outside* the church in the house, but that they were the ones inside the church in the house to whom Paul sent his *particular* greetings. Some people, besides being included in his general greetings to the church, needed special attention. Do not make the mistake of thinking that since everyone is included in the general greetings to the church, it is unnecessary to add further greetings to them individually. That is not holy affection; neither is it the fact. Paul did not do such a thing, and neither would you or I.

The proof of this is in verse 3. If the greeting sent to the church automatically included everyone and it was unnecessary to greet them again by mentioning certain names, Paul should not have greeted Prisca and Aquila in verse 3. Paul should have greeted in verse 5 just "the church, which is in their [Prisca and Aquila's] house." Should this not have included Prisca and Aquila already? Greeting the whole church naturally includes individuals. However, mentioning individuals in addition to greeting the church does not mean that these individuals *are not of the church but members of another group.* If this were so, then Prisca and Aquila *were not of the church that was in their own house!* Do you see the point? Paul greeted Prisca and Aquila in verse 3. Then in verse 5 he proceeded to greet the church which was in their house. If mentioning individual names in addition to greeting the church means that these individuals were not of this church and that there was another church in existence, then even Prisca and Aquila, whom Paul mentioned separately in his greeting, were not of the church which was in their own house!

The fact is that the church in the house of Prisca and Aquila *was* the church in Rome. The church in Rome at that time was in the house of Prisca and Aquila. Just as the individuals mentioned before verse 5, such as Prisca and Aquila, were of this church, so the many individuals named after verse 5 were also of this church. Moreover, the many individuals who were not mentioned were also of this same church.

In verses 10 and 11 two more houses are mentioned in which there were also the Lord's people. Nevertheless, Paul did not say, "Greet *the church* in Aristobulus's house" or "Greet *the church* in Narcissus's house." Only in verse 5 did Paul say, "Greet the church, which is in their [Prisca and Aquila's] house." Even though the whole household of Aristobulus believed in the Lord, there was only one church in Rome, which was the church that was in the house of Prisca and Aquila. Therefore, although there were believers of the household of Aristobulus, *they could not become the church.* Although many of Narcissus's household were believers, the believers in his house could not become an independent church. There was only one church in Rome, which was the church in the house of Prisca and Aquila. Therefore the Bible does not mention the church in the house of Narcissus. The household of Aquila, the household of Aristobulus, and the household of Narcissus all belonged to the church in Rome. Although these were three households of believers, there were not three churches. There was only one church. Rome was a locality; therefore, it had only one church, which was in the house of Prisca and Aquila.

History tells us that Rome was a very large city during the time of the Lord. But in the early days the believers in Rome were few. Because the city was large and the believers were scattered throughout the city, it was normal for Paul to add personal greetings to the greeting sent to the church in Rome, which was meeting in the house of Prisca and Aquila. He especially mentioned, "Greet Asyncritus, Phlegon, Hermes, Patrobas, Hermas, and the brothers with them" (v. 14), and also, "Greet Philologus and Julia, Nereus and his sister, and Olympas, and all the saints with them" (v. 15). These saints were scattered in places far away from each other in the city of Rome, just like the saints today in the church in Shanghai who live in the Yangshupu District or the region of Jiangwan. But Paul told us that there was only one church in the city of Rome and that was the one in the house of Prisca and Aquila. Although they were scattered and a few brothers were together with those who lived nearby, Paul *did not* call them the church; Paul only called them "the brothers with them" or "all the saints with them." Only one church can exist in one locality.

First Corinthians 16:19

"The churches of Asia greet you. Aquila and Prisca greet you much in the Lord with the church, which is in their house."

This salutation was given in A.D. 59 when Aquila and Prisca lived in Ephesus (Acts 18:18-19). The church in Ephesus was meeting in their house; it was therefore called "the church, which is in their house." This does not mean that one church was in the city of Ephesus and another church was in their house. It means that the church in the city of Ephesus *was* the church in the house of Aquila and Prisca. This historical fact cannot be changed.

Later, they returned to Rome and again opened their home to be the meeting place for the church in Rome. They were really a faithful and lovely couple.

Colossians 4:15-16

"Greet the brothers in Laodicea, as well as Nymphas and the church, which is in his house. And when this letter is read

among you, cause that it be read in the church of the
Laodiceans also."

We can discover from history that the church in Laodicea
met in the house of a brother by the name of Nymphas, a
believer in Laodicea, not Colossae. (Please refer to the writ-
ings of Moore, Alford, Earle, and Finley.) Therefore, Paul
called the church in Laodicea the church which was in
Nymphas's house, that is, the church in Laodicea in the house
of Nymphas. This is a fact, and it is very evident.

Question: Is it possible that "the brothers" mentioned in
verse 15 are different from the church?

Answer: No. How could it be possible? Paul mentions three
categories of people: 1) the brothers, 2) Nymphas, and 3) the
church. If the brothers and the church are not the same,
where does Nymphas fit in? It says, "The brothers...as well
as Nymphas." Does "the brothers" include "Nymphas" or not?
Everyone has to acknowledge that "the brothers" includes
"Nymphas." Therefore, both "the brothers" and "Nymphas"
are of the same group. Although both are of the same group,
after Paul had greeted the brothers (that is, after Nymphas
had been included in the greeting to the brothers), he especially singled out Nymphas and greeted him personally.

Furthermore, regarding "Nymphas" and "the church,
which is in his [Nymphas's] house," does the latter include the
former? Of course, the church has to include him. If so, why is
it not enough for Paul to say, "Greet the church, which is in
the house of Nymphas"? Although the church in his house
includes Nymphas, Paul still says, "Greet...Nymphas and the
church, which is in his house." He greets the church, but he
especially greets Nymphas.

In these three categories of people, Nymphas is a part of
each. In the same manner, "the brothers" and "the church" are
identical. Therefore, Paul does not stop with greeting "the
brothers in Laodicea," he goes on to greet a particular brother
by the name of "Nymphas." Since the meeting of the church is
in Nymphas's house, Paul therefore goes on to greet "the
church, which is in his house." "The brothers" refers to individuals, while the church refers to the whole group. But they

are identical. Paul first greets individuals, then greets the whole church.

Question: What is the relationship between "the church, which is in his house" in verse 15 and "the church of the Laodiceans" in verse 16?

Answer: Verse 15 is a greeting, while verse 16 regards the reading of the Epistle. In verse 15 Paul greets the brothers in Laodicea who are the church meeting in Nymphas's house. In verse 16 he spontaneously informs those at Colossae explicitly and without further explanation that the brothers in Laodicea whom he has greeted in verse 15 are the church that meets in Nymphas's house and that this church is the church in Laodicea. Now he requests that the brothers in Laodicea read his Epistle to the Colossians. (Colossae is only twelve miles away from Laodicea.) By reading these two verses carefully, you will see that the church in Nymphas's house in Laodicea (v. 15) is the very church of the Laodiceans (v. 16). Peter is Cephas, and Cephas is Peter—the two are interchangeable. The same is true here.

Philemon 1-2

"To Philemon...to Apphia...to Archippus...and to the church, which is in your house."

Philemon was a believer living in Colossae, and he was a co-worker of the apostle Paul. The church in Colossae met in his house; consequently, the phrase "to the church, which is in your house," indicates the church in Colossae. This is history.

Theotorian (?) said that until the fifth century, whenever visitors toured Colossae, they would visit the house of Philemon as a historical site. It was a place tourists could not miss in Colossae. This was due to the fact that the church in Colossae met in that particular house.

The church in the house of Philemon was *the church in Colossae,* for the church in Colossae met in the house of Philemon. Therefore, the churches in the Bible all take locality as the unit—the house can never be the unit for the church.

The House Being Insufficient as an Unit

We have seen that the New Testament speaks of the church in a house four times. What do all these actually mean? We must see whether or not the house is the unit for the jurisdiction of a church by examining this matter from another angle. I do not know whether or not you understand what a "unit of jurisdiction" means. For example, when we weigh things, we use the pound as the unit of measurement; thus, the pound is the "unit of weight." When we measure things, we use a foot as the unit. Thus, a foot is the "unit of length." A pound is a unit of weight, and a foot is a unit of length. Is a house the unit of jurisdiction for the church? As I have said before in other places, the unit of jurisdiction for the church is a city, or a locality. This is based upon God's teaching.

Why is it that a city, or a locality, is the unit? It is because Ephesus, Smyrna, Pergamos, Thyatira, Sardis, Philadelphia, and Laodicea were all localities, and only one church stood in each locality. If God did not take locality as the basic unit of church jurisdiction, there would not have been seven churches in these seven localities. There would have been instead one church for all seven localities. In other words, although one can say that there are seven localities, he cannot call the seven congregations in the seven localities seven churches (presuming that a church is not based on locality). But in the Bible, God told us that there were seven localities and *there were also seven churches!* They were seven churches in Asia, not the church in Asia; they were churches, not the church; they were the *ekklesiae,* not the *ekklesia.* Not only were there seven different churches on this earth, but there were also seven lampstands in the holy place before the Lord—there were seven, not one. It is undoubtedly evident that what men should obey is what God has shown us, that the locality should be the unit of jurisdiction for a church.

This is to say that a church takes a locality as its unit. When we add more than one unit together, we do not have just one unit; we must have two or more churches. Therefore, we have "the churches...in Judea [a province]" (1 Thes. 2:14) and "the churches of Galatia [a province]" (1 Cor. 16:1).

Because a province is made up of many localities and the basic unit of the church is a locality, once there are many localities, there are also many churches.

Again, may I ask, Can the house become the unit for the church? To answer this question, we must have a very clear mind; otherwise, we will make mistakes. We have to understand the difference between the house mentioned in the Bible and the house mentioned by those who advocate house churches today. The house that is spoken of in the Bible is the place where the church in that locality *met*. Therefore, the church in a certain person's house *is also* the church in that locality. The church in the house of Aquila *was* the church in Rome, the church in the house of Nymphas *was* the church in Laodicea, and the church in the house of Philemon *was* the church in Colossae.

What about today? Some people teach that although Rome is one locality, there can be two churches in Rome—one on a street and one in a house. They say that in Colossae there can be three churches—one on a street and two in different houses. They teach that the church in a house is a church that is smaller than the jurisdiction of a locality, and in the same locality there can be many churches. They utilize the word *house* in the Bible to assume that the church unit in the Scriptures is not limited or bound to a locality but to a house. You must take note that the house spoken of in the Bible and the house proposed by some people are entirely different.

Now the question is: In the Bible, is there a unit smaller than the locality for the boundary, the jurisdiction, of the church? Man says there is; God says there is not.

This question is very easy to answer. We have seen that there was only one church in Rome, one church in Colossae, and one church in Laodicea. Clearly, the book of Revelation shows us that the church in Laodicea was singular in number, which also corresponds to the one golden lampstand in the heavens.

The most obvious example was the church in Jerusalem, which at that time was the church with the greatest number of members. All those who study the Bible know that the meetings of the church in Jerusalem were held in different homes. The Bible says, "In the temple and...from house to house" (Acts 2:46). The word *house* here is not merely one house. Acts 5:42 also records, "...in the temple and from house to house." Here again it is not merely one house. Later, when Peter came out of prison, he went to the "house of Mary" (12:12), which was one among many of the houses. Now the question is whether this kind of house can be the unit of jurisdiction for the church. History shows us that among all the other churches, Jerusalem had the greatest number of members and the greatest number of home meetings. If God had any intention to take the house as the church unit, then Jerusalem would have been the most qualified locality and the best church to be a pattern to others. If in Jerusalem, where there were many members and many houses, God did not use the house to be the sphere, the jurisdiction of the church, then we know it is not likely to find any factual basis for taking a house as the sphere of the church elsewhere in the Bible.

What then is the fact? There were many houses in Jerusalem, but God had *only one church* in Jerusalem. Every time the Holy Spirit speaks of the church in Jerusalem, He consistently uses the word *church* in the singular, never *churches* in the plural. The Bible only uses the term *the church in Jerusalem*, never *the churches in Jerusalem*. It never says, "Every church in every house in Jerusalem." There may have been many houses for meetings, but there was still one church in Jerusalem. Any thought of taking the house as the unit of the church is a human concept, not the teaching of the Bible. Just this one phrase "the church which was in Jerusalem" (Acts 8:1) is enough to make it impossible for anyone to establish an isolated, independent, individual, and solitary church in a house.

We also can compare Acts 14:23 with Titus 1:5: "...appointed elders for them in every church" and "...appoint elders in every city." These two verses correspond and agree with each other. "Every church" is in "every city." It is in every city, not in every house. The house may be used as a meeting place, and the church may be called the church in a certain person's house. However, the church in Nymphas's house was still the church in Laodicea. The city or the locality, not the house, is the proper designation of a church; it is the proper boundary of the church and the proper unit of the church.

Two Mistakes

Two great mistakes are found in men today.

First, some people desire to have a church bigger than a city or a locality. They want to unite many churches in different localities and make them one big church, that is, bigger than a locality. They have never considered that there is not such a term like *the church in China* in the Scriptures. How many realize that the term *the church in China* is not scriptural? All of God's children must understand that in the Scriptures there is not a united church that is greater than a locality.

It is "the *churches* of Galatia [a province]" (Gal. 1:2), not "the church of Galatia."

It is "the *churches* of the Gentiles" (Rom. 16:4), not "the church of the Gentiles."

It is "the *churches*...which are in Judea [a province]" (1 Thes. 2:14), not "the church in Judea."

It is "the *seven churches* which are in Asia [a province]" (Rev. 1:4), not "the church in Asia."

It is "*the churches*" in Syria and Cilicia [districts], not "the church" in Syria and Cilicia (Acts 15:41).

Therefore, the boundary, the jurisdiction, of the church on the earth is limited to a locality. Even if we put two churches in two different localities together, they cannot be one church; they are still two churches. In the province of Asia, if we add up the churches as one plus one plus one plus one plus one plus one plus one, the result is not one church, but seven churches. In the whole province of Galatia, if all the churches in the different localities are added together, we still will not have the church in Galatia, but "the churches of Galatia." Who can say that the church is over and above the locality? May God open our eyes so that we will not cause confusion to the testimony of God.

Second, some people desire to have a church smaller than the city or the locality. They want to divide one locality into

many "churches," many "assemblies," or many "congregations." Some euphemize these gatherings as "house churches."
But these are all of the same nature. They are divisions, the
purpose of which is to establish men's own sects according to
the flesh. God's children must discriminate between the
house spoken of in the Bible and the house as it is conceived
in human thought. In the Bible, when the house is equivalent
to a locality or city, that house is called the church, like the
church in Rome, the church in Colossae, the church in
Laodicea, etc. But when the house is smaller than the locality
or city, that house cannot be called the church, like the house
meetings of the church in Jerusalem. This is very different
from the house conceived in human thought, which is purposely made smaller than the locality or city, perpetuating
the life of the sects or changing the sects into another form.

The brothers, therefore, must remember the teachings of
the Bible:

It is "the church which was in Jerusalem" (Acts 8:1), not
"the churches in Jerusalem."

It is "the church...which is in Corinth" (1 Cor. 1:2), not
"the four churches in Corinth."

It is "the church in Laodicea" (Rev. 3:14; Col. 4:15-16), not
"the two churches in Laodicea."

There is "the church in Ephesus," not "the churches in
Ephesus." There is "the church of the Thessalonians," not "the
churches of the Thessalonians." There is "the church in
Antioch," not "the churches in Antioch."

God's church takes locality as its boundary. When the
church in a certain person's house is completely equivalent to
the church of that locality, it can be called the church in that
person's house. However, when the "church" in a certain
person's house is smaller than the church in his locality, it
cannot be called a church. If the "churches" in the "house"
of Cephas, in the "house" of Paul, in the "house" of Apollos,
and in the "house" of Christ were added together, there would
not be *four* churches in Corinth, they would still singularly be
the church in Corinth. From this we can see that God has
never made this type of "house" a unit for the boundary, the
jurisdiction, of the church. Since the four houses are not four

units, the believers meeting in them respectively cannot be four churches.

There must have been over ten thousand brothers in Jerusalem, and they might have been divided into one hundred houses for meetings. Since houses of this kind are smaller than the city, that is, smaller than the locality, and smaller than Jerusalem, they are not sufficient to become the units of the church. If we add these one hundred houses together, they do not become one hundred churches. In the Bible there is only the singular church in Jerusalem. Since one hundred meetings added together could not become one hundred churches, but only one, this means that each one is not sufficient to become a unit by itself.

If the church in Nymphas's house (Col. 4:15) and the church in Laodicea (v. 16) are not the same, then when we add them up they must be *two* churches, but after we add "them" together in this way, God speaks of "the church in Laodicea" in Revelation 3:14, not "the churches" or "the two churches in Laodicea." They are just one.

When the house is smaller than a locality, it is not sufficient to become a unit. When the house is equivalent to the locality, it is qualified to become a unit. But the unit is the locality, not the house. We must be very clear that the standard unit for the boundary of the church in the Bible is the city or locality. When the house is equivalent to the locality, we can speak of the church in So-and-so's house. When the house is smaller than the locality, we can add one plus one, but the total is not two; it is still one. We may add ten plus ten, but the total is not twenty; it is one. We may add one hundred plus one hundred, but the total is not two hundred; it is only one. The total is always one. By this we know that a "house" cannot equal the unit for the boundary, the jurisdiction, of the church.

Who can point out from the Bible two churches in one locality? No one! I can only say that one locality has two denominations, or one locality has four sects, or one hundred localities have more than one hundred manifestations of the flesh. But I cannot say that one locality has two or more churches. I can only say that one locality has over one hundred home meetings. One locality only has one church. This is certain.

For the past twenty-eight years, as a result of the Lord's calling, the denominations have lost their place in the heart of those who love the Lord. The brothers who recommend dividing the church into houses must guard against the suspicion that they are changing things for the sake of defending the sects or themselves. May the Lord cause His children to see that all those who have left the denominations have not necessarily left the sects. May God have mercy on me for speaking frankly.

We must seriously ask our hearts in the light: Am I rejecting the sin of denominations on the one hand, while refusing to "submit to the church" on the other hand, and by so doing have I only come up with the compromise of the house? May the Lord have mercy on those who do this, and may He have mercy on me for speaking it.

I am very sad at heart because at the critical moment when the Lord is moving on victoriously, such a disruption has come in. If we are only slightly disobedient today, a hundred years from now—should the Lord delay His coming—this disobedience will become a great detour for the church. I hope you brothers would fast and pray for our brothers. May God turn back their hearts. On the other hand, those who have contact with them must demonstrate firm and unchanging love so that the Lord could gain back these ones. May the Lord put a fear and a trembling in them. May they know that speaking for the Lord requires the putting aside of oneself. They should be humble, and they should see and listen before speaking. May they also see the serious result of speaking without revelation. Once Ishmael is born, the fleshly will forever persecute the spiritual. This is going on all the time, even until today (Gal. 4:29).

The Impossibility of Having It Both Ways

Some people have a wrong thought. They agree that the boundary, the jurisdiction, of the church is locality, yet because they are unwilling to get out of the sects, they think that the house is also a boundary of the church. They think the two can go together side by side without contradiction. They cannot distinguish when the house is the same as the locality and when the house is different from the locality. When the house is the same as the locality, it can be the boundary of the church. When the house is different from the locality, the two cannot be the boundary, the unit, of the church at the same time. The key rests with locality, whether or not the house equals the locality.

If the house is the unit, then locality, which is bigger than the house, cannot be the unit. How can locality be the unit if it can be divided into smaller units? If we acknowledge locality as the unit, how can we *also* acknowledge the house as a unit? Since locality is the smallest unit, how can it be divided into smaller units such as houses? (Please remember that those who promote "house" churches do not view the word *house* scripturally; that is, they do not consider house in the context that locality and house are identical. Instead, they view the house according to their own concept, making it smaller than locality. This is not the kind of house spoken of in the Bible. Please pay attention to this matter.) If a foot is one unit of measure, then an inch is not sufficient to be the unit, because it is less than a full unit. If we take an inch to be the unit, a foot can no longer be the unit, because a foot equals twelve units. Likewise, if the unit for the church is locality, then the many houses in one locality cannot be many churches. One locality with one house has but one church; one locality with one hundred houses also has but one church. With one hundred houses there are not one hundred churches. If the house is the unit, then there is one church with one house, and there are one hundred churches with one hundred houses. In this case a locality with one hundred houses could never have only one church. These two, house and locality, are completely different units. Either we take the house as the unit or locality as the unit. There must be a unit, but we cannot have both. The house and the locality cannot both be units for the church.

If the locality is the unit, then 1) a united church of several localities joined together is wrong, and 2) isolated divisions within one locality are also wrong. If the house is the unit, then 1) the united church is still wrong, but 2) the divisions in each locality are justified. All the divisions within a locality can hide behind the word *house*. If the "house" is the unit, all who refuse "to hear the church" (Matt. 18:17) can organize separate "house" churches. The "house" church becomes a shelter to all the divisive ones in a locality. May the Lord be merciful to His church.

Therefore, we must be clear that there can be only one unit—either house or locality, not both of them together. Similarly, if our salvation is not by grace, it has to be by works. It cannot be by grace and works; we cannot have both. According to the Bible, the boundary, the jurisdiction, of the church is the locality, just as our salvation is by grace. Dividing the church in a locality into many "house" churches brings divisions into the Body. It is the work of the flesh.

I believe God in His great wisdom made the locality the boundary of the church in order to eliminate the works of man, which try to divide the church within one locality.

The Intention and the Outcome

When we search the Bible for judgment and settlement upon some teaching, we must not only check the intention of our heart, but we must also take heed to the direction in which this kind of teaching leads and the outcome it produces.

For example, someone said that the Bible never prohibits Christians from smoking opium. He said, "If you say that Christians should not smoke opium, please prove it from the Bible." Undoubtedly, the Bible does not have clearly written statements prohibiting the smoking of opium. But we must take note of the outcome that this kind of saying will bring to the children of God. The only thing this teaching will do is lead men into the world and to fulfill their lusts. Another example is baptism. Some think that immersion is right, but sprinkling is also right. They give many reasons for their position. But these reasons simply reveal that man can change God's word. Likewise, if anyone says that there can be the church in a house besides the church in a locality, we will also ask, What will be the outcome of this kind of teaching? Could there be any other outcome than that of men within a locality having the freedom in the flesh to break the unity of the church and to lead God's children into the way of divisions? If in one locality there can be many "house" churches, with all having their own administration and thinking that they are one spiritually, are they not deceiving themselves? If we maintain this kind of teaching, how many more divisions will result in a locality, divisions under the name of so-called "house" churches? At present there are already scores of denominational churches, but if "house" churches are scriptural, there will be hundreds more churches in one locality! Is this something that a person who has consecrated himself to the Lord and who loves the Lord would want to see?

We all know there is only one church. Throughout history, past and present, there is only one church. Because there is only one Head, there is only one Body. The church is a Body with life; thus, it is not right to divide it *for any reason*. We must stress this: The church is one because the Body is one. Any excuse to divide the church is a sin. Division is sin, because it is a "division in the body" (1 Cor. 12:25).

Although the church is one, it is impossible for all the brothers to meet together. Time and space prevent all the brothers around the whole world from meeting together all the time. Besides this, it is impractical as far as church administration, supervision, and management are concerned for all the brothers to come together in one world church. Therefore, God's Word not only permits but also ordains that the church be separated. In order to practically make the church (singular) become the churches (plural), God has established the way for one individual church and another individual church to remain two churches instead of one. This is the principle of "locality" as revealed in the Bible.

In the Bible no church is bigger than the locality; neither is any church smaller than the locality. Whenever people gather and dwell together, there is a "locality." A locality is where people gather and dwell together. As long as a locality is a place where people gather and dwell together, it is the boundary of the church according to the Bible. People who dwell together in one locality can be independent of other localities. It is not a matter of the number of people

THE CHURCH IN THE CITY AND IN THE HOUSE

(believers), but a matter of locality. The basis for separation is not love or lack of love, but locality. The basis for God allowing the church to be separated is locality. Any other kind of separation is sin. We commit sin if we are separated from our brothers for any other reason than that of locality. In the Bible the only kind of distinction that does not touch upon the nature of the church is the distinction of locality. The distinction of locality is God's great wisdom. I am in Shanghai and you are in Soochow, but when we both come to Nanking, we will not create any problem. Other than the boundary of locality, there absolutely should be no other boundary. In the church God only allows us to separate by the principle of locality.

Undoubtedly the church is one. How then can there be many churches? The distinction can only be on the basis of locality. Because we have our physical body, we are naturally limited by geographical boundaries. Any difference because of names, human feelings, or other factors is harmful to the nature of the church. Only the distinction of locality does not touch the nature of the church. In this way, no one can turn away from the general ground of locality. We may be able to do many things, but we are not qualified to establish a church as we like. Once we see that the ground of the church is local, there will be no more reason for the existence of any sects. The matter of locality cuts man's flesh to the deepest part.

Now let me repeat what I have been saying about the nature of the church. Any reason to divide the church damages the nature of the church; that is, it turns the unity of the church into disunity. Due to the fact that we are in the human body, geography is the only factor that can separate us. Such separation does not threaten the nature of church unity. Therefore, God ordained to have locality as the earthly boundary of the church. God also ordained that in one locality there should be only one church to express the unity of the heavenly church.

We must see the spiritual reason for separating the church by localities. Once we see this, we will know whether or not the present-day principle of separating the church by houses is of God. The way to separate the saints at Jerusalem

by houses was scriptural. Due to the great number of people—
a physical reality—they were separated into many meetings
in the houses. The church, however, was still one, "the church
[singular number] in Jerusalem." Today, man's way to divide
the church by houses is to make many churches within one
locality. It has nothing to do with physical limitations, geographical reasons, or the inconvenience of coming together
from great distances. It has nothing to do with the fact that
the crowd is large and that there is not enough room to sit
together. It has nothing to do with the fact that there are so
many people and that care for them is impossible. It has
nothing to do with the practical problem of handling administration over great distances. It is simply a way of dividing the
church into many churches. Dividing people into many
churches because of such an underlying reason is harmful to
the nature of the church. Separations that are not based on
geographical or physical demand are spiritual in nature; they
touch the spiritual unity. This kind of separation is not outward and limited, but inward and spiritual. Any division that
is not for a geographical or physical reason is an intrinsic,
real, basic, and spiritual division. Therefore, this kind of division is a division in the very nature and essence of the
church. It is damaging to the spiritual unity.

This is very serious. Since we first saw the light concerning the oneness of the Body of Christ twenty-eight years ago,
we have passed through many waves of adversity. But I
believe we have never passed through one that is more serious and more ambiguous than the teaching about the "house"
church. This is the first time people have opposed the truth
by agreeing with it. Since we all are people who serve God, I
beg you to seek the light of God. Do not send forth a confusing
voice in the church of God; rather get rid of the sectarianism
from your heart.

We must not push the oneness of the church entirely to the
"spiritual" side by saying, "We are one in life! We are one spiritually!" Brothers, when we do not live together in the same
city, we might be able to cover ourselves with spiritual words
and hide our disunity with such "spiritual oneness." But since
we all live in the same city, is it conceivable that we would not

express or demonstrate our oneness? Since there are no geographical and physical factors to divide us, is not this the time to show that we are one church? Why at such an opportune time for us to show our oneness should this different teaching related to a "house" church come into being? Does this teaching related to a "house" church represent unity or separation and sectarianism? Lord, have mercy on us!

I dare not say from where the teaching about the "house" church comes. But I am afraid that the brother who speaks about this has not seen the sin of sects. This teaching is a halfway place to sectarianism; it is not a thorough rejection of sects. A person who has left the denominations is not necessarily one who has left the sects. I am afraid that some who only know their individual movement, individual living, and individual work are not willing to be limited by the Body. These are the ones who love this kind of talk about the "house" church. Those who do not desire to listen to the church but desire to establish their own churches value this kind of "doctrine." May the Lord's blood cover me for speaking like this. I think humility may be profitable to some people, but not to take our own way is profitable to all of God's children.

Finally, this kind of "house" church is not the house that is in the Scriptures. This kind of "house" church is a sect, a disguised sect. This kind of "house" church causes people to divide, not to unite. This kind of "house" church hurts the nature of the church while concealing its wound. This kind of "house" church builds up the individualism, lawlessness, and ambition for leadership in many. May the Lord have mercy on me for speaking in such a way. May He have mercy on His churches that they may not be damaged.

CHAPTER THREE

THE CONTENT OF THE CHURCH

(A talk to the brothers and sisters in Shanghai on December 4, 1950, published in *The Open Door,* dated March 1, 1951.)

I would like to speak to the brothers a little more concerning the problem of the church. The church must have both the authority of the Spirit and the ground of locality. The ground of locality, however, is not a simple matter, because a church still needs content. Without content, it still cannot be regarded as a local church. Being correct in name is a very important matter, but being correct in name does not necessarily mean that there is no problem. This is the reason I would like to see from the Bible, together with you, several requirements of a church in a locality. Just saying that we are standing on the ground of locality is not enough. In order to say that a church is standing on the ground of locality, it should fulfill certain requirements and conditions and should have a certain content. If none of these requirements and conditions are met, we are still not standing on the ground of locality.

Receptive

First, if a church is really standing on the ground of locality as set forth in the Bible, she must receive all whom the Lord has received. Romans 15:7 says, "Therefore receive one another, as Christ also received you to the glory of God." Here we see one thing: The receiving of a Christian is based upon the receiving of Christ—that is, we should receive one another as Christ has received us. In other words, we cannot refuse those whom Christ has received. If a sinner has been received by Christ, we must receive him as a brother. If we do not receive a man whom Christ has received, immediately we are a sect, not the church.

What is a church? A church receives all whom Christ has received in one locality. God is not as concerned with those who live in Shanghai receiving the brothers in Nanking or Chungking as He is about them receiving the brothers in their locality. We must receive all whom Christ has received. If we want to determine whether or not the church in Tientsin is a church, all we have to do is see whether or not it receives all those who are saved in Tientsin. Suppose the brothers in Tientsin want to be selective; they only want to receive a certain type of people who have been received by Christ and not another type of people who also have been received by Christ. Then that is not the church. We cannot say that we receive those who are the same as us, while we do not receive those who are not the same as us. We cannot fail to receive one whom the Lord has received for any reason; otherwise, we are not the church.

"Him who is weak in faith receive,... for God has received him" (Rom. 14:1, 3). Suppose someone is a vegetarian. We may consider that he is very weak. However, the basis for receiving is whether or not God has received him, not whether he is strong or weak. Perhaps he is a weak brother, but we still must receive him. God already has received him without regard for his strength or weakness; therefore, we must receive him as well. The fundamental fellowship of a church in a locality is based upon the fellowship of God. We must receive a brother whom God has received. We cannot have any reason to refuse him; otherwise, we are a sect, not a church. The church in a locality is based on a receiving that is as broad as God and also as strict as God: Whomever God receives, we receive; whomever God does not receive, we do not receive. The universal church receives all whom God has received in the whole world; a local church receives all whom God has received in a locality. No matter how different a brother is from us or how far short he is of our standard, there is only one requirement for us to receive him—that is, has God received him? If God has received him, we must receive him. Therefore, a local church—we must be very clear about this—must take the life of Christ and faith in God as the basis for receiving believers. Apart from this we do not have any other demands. If we make other demands as certain requirements, we are a sect just like any other sect. A sect is condemned and is therefore a very serious matter.

Exercising Discipline

Does this mean that we must receive all believers in a locality without any reservations? No! A church in a locality must not only receive all whom Christ has received in that locality, but must also exercise church discipline. What is this discipline? When a brother who has been received by the Lord commits something that requires the Lord to exclude him from fellowship, we too must exercise discipline upon him. We should not say that we want all whom the Lord wants and all whom the Lord does not want. If the Lord puts a certain one into the world, yet we put him into the church, we open a door to the world in the church. As a result, there will be no boundary between the church and the world; the wall between them will be torn down by us.

We often use this illustration: When a boat is at sea, the boat and the sea cannot have fellowship. As soon as they begin to have fellowship, the boat will begin to sink into the sea. Likewise, if a hole is drilled in the church, the line of separation between the church and the world will disappear. Therefore, the local church must exercise discipline; it must have disciplinary action in order to be a local church.

What is disciplinary action? First Corinthians 5 speaks of six different kinds of persons who are saved and have God's life, but they have indulged themselves and become a fornicator, a covetous man, a reviler, a drunkard, an idolater, and an extortioner (v. 11). Paul told the church in Corinth to "remove the evil man from among yourselves" (v. 13). The command in 1 Corinthians 5 does not say that we must put a brother away from among us as soon as he has sinned. But it does say that we must put him away when he becomes *such a one*. It does not say one who commits fornication, but "a fornicator"; not a brother who reviles, but "a reviler." When a man becomes such a one, the church must put him away; it must excommunicate him. Whomever the Lord does not want in the church, we also must not want in the church. If we keep one whom the Lord does not want in our locality, this retention will cause trouble. The Lord said that such a one is like a little leaven which will leaven the whole lump (1 Cor. 5:6). Before long, the whole church will be moldy. The whole church will no longer be pure flour; it will have leaven. Therefore, the church must have discipline. Moreover, the church knows what kind of person a brother is. This is reflected in the words of Sister M. E. Barber: "The oneness of the church is the voice of the Holy Spirit." If all the brothers feel that a brother is such a person, then it is certain that he is such a person. We cannot say that all the brothers have misunderstood him. Therefore, a local church must execute God's discipline in its locality.

Furthermore, the Bible reveals that the church executes discipline in regard to not only moral issues but also doctrinal issues. However, the Lord does not want us to exercise discipline regarding ordinary doctrines. For example, some keep the Lord's Day while others keep the Sabbath. (This does not refer to the Seventh-day Adventists, who are recovering the law.) Some keep both days; we should not argue about this. Some brothers eat vegetables and some eat meat; we should not argue about this. However, there is a kind of doctrine which we must defend by all means, and that is the doctrine concerning *the person of the Lord Jesus*. This is mentioned in 2 John 7 through 11:

> For many deceivers went out into the world, those
> who do not confess Jesus Christ coming in the flesh.
> This is the deceiver and the antichrist.... Everyone
> who goes beyond and does not abide in the teaching
> of Christ does not have God.... If anyone comes to
> you and does not bring this teaching, do not receive
> him into your house, and do not say to him, Rejoice!
> For he who says to him, Rejoice, shares in his evil
> works.

Here I think it is very clear that a church in a locality must uphold the person of the Lord Jesus. If the Lord Jesus is not God manifest in the flesh, that is, if He is only flesh, then He is not God, and the Lord Jesus could not have accomplished redemption for us. The church, therefore, would be basically annulled. Therefore, the church must be strict about anything that concerns the person of Christ. It must not be loose or lenient at all in this matter. If someone preaches a different teaching about the person of the Lord, do not receive him into your house and do not say to him, Rejoice. Otherwise, your church will lose its ground. As long as it has no discipline, it loses its qualification as a church. Moral confusion is wrong and not allowed by the church, and doctrinal confusion is also wrong and not allowed by the church. However, we should by no means identify differences over ordinary doctrines as being included in this category. If the church deals with ordinary doctrines as it deals with such confusion, the whole church will be cut up and divided into pieces. We should not argue about ordinary doctrines. We must only defend the doctrines regarding the person of Christ. Here the church must exercise discipline; otherwise, the church is finished.

Matthew 18:15-17 says, "Moreover if your brother sins against you, go, reprove him between you and him alone.... But if he does not hear you, take with you one or two more....And if he refuses to hear them, tell it to the church; and if he refuses to hear the church also, let him be to you just like the Gentile." Some churches are very lazy and do not care to handle troublesome matters. But the Lord said that the church must take care of disciplinary matters, if it is to be a church at all. The Lord's teaching in chapter eighteen is regarding the local church because it refers to a place in which we can "tell." The local church must take care of these matters. If a local church does not take care of these matters, she is neglecting her duty. If we are a church in a locality, we must bear all the responsibility in that locality.

Inclusive

Furthermore, the most important matter for the church in a locality is that she must be inclusive, not exclusive. The church must be inclusive in two aspects of its behavior and its doctrine. First, we will consider the aspect of Christian behavior that the church should not exclude.

In Acts 20:27 Paul told the elders of Ephesus, "I did not shrink from declaring to you all the counsel of God," or "I did not shrink from declaring to you the *perfect, complete* will of God." If the church in a locality is standing in the position of the church, she must not shrink from declaring the perfect, complete will of God. We cannot expect that every brother will touch the perfect, complete will of God, but like Paul we must not shrink from or reject one truth concerning the perfect, complete will of God. As soon as we shy away from some aspect of the truth, we are a sect. If we exclude those who believe in the certain truths which we shrink from, then we are not able to include all of God's children.

"The church...is His Body, the fullness of the One who fills all in all" (Eph. 1:22-23). The Lord fills the universal church; the Lord also fills the local church. If a local church only has a part of Christ, that is not the church. The church is the Body of Christ, which means the whole Christ. For example, if my waist is forty inches around and I am given a suit with a waistline measuring thirty inches, I will not be able to wear it. The clothing must be big enough for me to wear. The relationship of the church to Christ is like the body to life; it is not exactly like clothing to the body. Sometimes we can force our clothing a little to fit our body, but we can never force our body to contain life. The Body must be complete in order to fully contain the whole life of Christ. Only when the Lord's fullness is in the church in Shanghai can it be called the church in Shanghai. If the church allows a certain matter but disallows another matter, then the church has a shortage. If there is anything that we cannot accept, the portion of Christ within that very thing will be excluded from us. In such a case, we are not perfectly complete; the church is maimed. This is very important. The church is filled with the fullness of Christ. The church is the Body of Christ; Christ puts on such a church as His outward container. The church must be large enough to contain Christ. The church must have a large enough shell for Christ to fit into. If the church does not have all that His life has, the church cannot express the complete Christ and cannot be called the church.

Colossians 1:25 says, "Of which I became a minister according to the stewardship of God, which was given to me for you, to complete the word of God." Within the church, there must be the complete word of God. The word of God must be completed in the church. After reading these words, we may not understand the practical side. For example, what does it mean to have the word of God and all kinds of scriptural behavior fulfilled in the church? What does it mean that a local church should be inclusive and not exclusive?

(1) As an example, we have been talking about the matter of spiritual gifts in these days. We say that we are the church in Shanghai, but suppose that brothers in Shanghai do not believe in spiritual gifts. Is this all right? No! The church cannot say that it does not believe in spiritual gifts, because there are spiritual gifts in the Bible. As soon as we do not believe in spiritual gifts, we cannot be the church in Shanghai; we can only be called "a church in Shanghai that does not believe in spiritual gifts." Our refusal to believe in spiritual gifts causes us not to be inclusive and makes us exclusive to some brothers. Suppose there are twenty brothers in Shanghai who believe in spiritual gifts. Once we refuse to believe in spiritual gifts, we cannot include them; we keep them out. Since they are members of the Body of Christ, our excluding of them may not be like cutting off our hand, but at least it is like cutting off a finger. Therefore, we cannot say that this church is filled with the fullness of Christ. We have not fulfilled the word of God; we have cut off a portion of Christ.

(2) Consider a greater matter, such as selling all to follow the Lord. Suppose the brothers in Shanghai do not believe in selling everything, but instead believe in working diligently to earn money and taking out a certain percentage of it for distribution to the poor. If one hundred brothers in Shanghai are moved by the Spirit of the Lord to sell everything and follow the Lord, they will feel that there is no place for them in this church. If we have no way to include them, we are exclusive to them. But selling all to follow the Lord is a part of the life of Christ. If we cannot include the brothers who have this portion of life, if we ostracize them, we can see that our church is both too small and it is maimed. This is like amputating a hand or foot. How can the church not have all

that Christ has? If the church does not have all that Christ has, this church cannot stand in the position of the church. It is a sect, not a church. A church must include the fullness of Christ. If it does not, these one hundred brothers will eventually form a church that sells all to follow the Lord, bringing forth one more sect. We will not be complete and neither will they. Our doctrine is not broad enough to include them, and theirs is also not the perfect, complete will of God. We cut them off, and they also cut us off.

Therefore, a local church must include all kinds of God's children who seek the Lord. It must include the brothers who sell everything as well as the brothers who do not sell everything. We cannot include what is not in the Bible; otherwise, we will include the world. But we must include what is in the Bible; otherwise, we will separate and exclude some of God's children.

Acts 5:4 says, "While it [the property] remained, was it not your own?" It is evident that before the property was sold, it could remain the owners'. The Bible shows us that there were believers who did not sell everything; they all could still be Christians. If a certain group is unwilling to admit those who do not sell all, it is a "family" (as practiced by some Christians in China), not the church. Ordinary denominations do not require everyone to sell all, but the "family" does require this; therefore, they also are not the church. Anything that bars a part of God's children is exclusive and sectarian. It is best for all the brothers to take the path of completeness. If we are not able to climb up this way, we should not hinder others from doing so. This is the only way for us to be inclusive and to be called the church. It is best for all God's servants to come up to this standard. If we are not able, we must reserve the path for others to take. What the Bible permits, we must permit; what the Bible does not permit, we also must not permit. We must have the aspiration to climb higher; we must take this road no matter how difficult. But even if we cannot make it, we must still allow other brothers the liberty to take this way. The church should never include only what we can do and exclude what we cannot do. We are not large enough to be the standard; we cannot be the basis for forming any kind of judgment.

Andrew Murray once said, "We who are the Lord's servants sooner or later will have to preach words which we are unable to fulfill." We should never hinder others from going on because we cannot go on. The church in a locality must have this kind of broad-mindedness in order to stand in the position of the church. This may seem strange, but this is a fact. Paul's walk was in accord with everything he preached, but people like us still have to preach even if we are not able to go on accordingly.

(3) Another example involves taking medicine when one is sick. There is a scriptural basis for this because Luke continued to work as a physician after he was saved. During times of sickness, it is all right to take something to help the body. Some brothers, however, only look to the Lord when they are sick; they take no medicine at all. The proper attitude of the church should include both. If brothers are able to believe in divine healing without the help of a doctor or medicine, this is best. If some brothers are short in faith and consult a doctor and take some medicine, this is also all right. If a group of brothers believe in science and think it is too much for others to refuse medicine and reject those who do, this group of brothers immediately will exclude some brothers and drive them out. However, we must not go to the other extreme, insisting on not seeing a doctor or not taking medicine like the former "Mount Zion Church." If we do, those who are short in faith may be put to death by us.

On the west side of Egypt, along the Sudan, malaria was very prevalent. Many brothers who believed in divine healing went there and said, "Quinine is medicine; we will not take it." As a result, every year scores out of a hundred died. But another group of brothers said, "In this place quinine is food, not medicine." As a result, only a few in a hundred died yearly. Evidently, the proposal of the first group was wrong.

Basically, our attitude should be to not bring in what is not permitted in the Bible, but to include whatever is permitted in the Bible. This is the way to be inclusive, not exclusive. We should not say that we must depend on medicine. If we do, those who believe in divine healing will go away. We also should not insist on avoiding medicine; otherwise, those who are weak in faith will go away. A church must be inclusive, not exclusive. All sects are the result of failure in this matter. We must give our attention to this.

(4) Regarding the matter of holiness, many of God's children believe that once they believe in the Lord they are perfect. Other children of God believe that they still need the second blessing in order to be perfect. In the Bible some were made perfect once they were blessed, but some also were blessed a second or third time before they touched perfection. Because the Brethren believe in perfection by being blessed once, the Holiness brothers leave because they absolutely believe that perfection is gained in the second blessing. But since they absolutely believe in the second blessing for perfection, the Brethren brothers leave because they believe in perfection by being blessed once. If a church picks only the Scriptures it believes in, it is not standing in the position of the church but, in fact, in the position of a denomination. We preach both the doctrine of perfection by being blessed once and the doctrine of perfection by receiving a second blessing. We can lead people to be made perfect by being blessed once, and we also can lead people to be liberated by receiving a second blessing. Whether or not we will bring forth more sects in the future depends upon whether or not we have reserved a place for all of God's children. If we have not reserved a place for all of God's children, we are a sect.

(5) Now I will mention several outward matters. For example, head covering is definitely in the Bible. Today the church must be absolutely in favor of head covering. But if some brothers have not seen it, we have to take the attitude of Romans 14 and wait for them to see it, because we must receive those whom the Lord receives. Although they do not see it, we hope they will see it in the future. The church can only stand on the positive side of what is in the Bible, not on the negative side. If some have not seen the matter of head covering, the church can only say that they will be received in spite of their weak faith. If a sister covers her head and the church does not receive her, she will feel that the church is

not hers and she will leave. Then we will force a head-covering sect to be brought forth. If we stand in the position of not favoring head covering and do not allow the sisters to cover their heads, we are not a church. Receiving the saints is not based on whether or not sisters cover their heads. If the brothers' receiving is based upon head covering rather than Christ's receiving, the sisters who cover their heads will think that this church is not theirs. Therefore, we clearly must see that we have to stand on the side of what is in the Bible. If there are some who are unable to come up to this, we must also forbear them.

(6) The matter of laying on of hands is also found in the Bible. Some brothers are not able to go on with this matter, and we should not insist that they do. However, if we do not practice what is in the Bible, some brothers will leave us. Those who oppose the laying on of hands are a sect, a sect of "the non-laying on of hands." If we want to stand in the position of the church, we must accept whatever is in the Word of God.

(7) Baptism is argued about the most. Why has there been so much argument about this matter over the last several hundred years? This is because some have brought things from Roman Catholicism into Protestantism. Since Roman Catholicism sprinkled water on people's heads, many Protestant churches did the same. Originally, both sides probably exercised some forebearance and went through much discussion. But in the end each went its own way. With any command of the Bible, whenever the church does not stand on the positive side to maintain what is in the Bible, a sect is created.

(8) Concerning the matter of breaking of bread, the Bible speaks of remembering the Lord on the first day of every week. If certain churches do not practice this according to the Bible, those who want to remember the Lord this way can only leave.

(9) Foot-washing is also in the Bible. Some radically oppose this matter and bring it to nothing by their teaching. Consequently, those who want to obey the Lord's command in foot-washing leave.

(10) Among God's children, some stress teaching, others stress deeper life, and still others stress gospel preaching. Brothers who are zealous in preaching the gospel often look down upon those who stress the deeper life, and brothers who stress the deeper life often look down upon those who preach the gospel. When you look down upon me and I look down upon you, divisions immediately appear.

(11) I will give another example. Some brothers emphasize preaching by inspiration. Of course, this is very rare. They preach by the inspiration that comes from spiritual gifts. This is very good. This is the kind of prophesying spoken of in 1 Corinthians 14. These brothers are not in favor of expounding the Bible. But is this not in the Bible? In the Bible there are those who preach the gospel and those who teach. If some brothers disapprove of expounding the Bible, those who study the Bible will find it unbearable. Those who are teachers will leave. But if the church only believes in teaching by expounding the Scriptures, those who believe in inspiration will not be able to tolerate it. Then divisions will result.

The entire difficulty is that we are too small! Our heart is not broad enough before the Lord, and our person is not big enough. "I want this, and I do not want that; the church must be managed according to my idea." Please remember, the church is managed according to the Lord's will, not according to our ideas, because we are too small. There are always some brothers better than us in certain aspects; we cannot say that we are superior to all the brothers. There are always some brothers and sisters who are above us in certain points. We cannot run ahead of them all. We must learn to receive the good points of all the brothers because only the Lord is equivalent to a church. Only when the whole church is added up will it equal one Lord. Even if we have received special mercy of the Lord, we can only equal a portion; we cannot equal all the brothers. If we equal two or twenty brothers, that is the Lord's mercy. But if we think we equal the whole church, what kind of pride is this? How can we make every brother like us? If every brother and sister is like us, the church has no future. Surely, many brothers and sisters are ahead of us in many areas. The church is one-sided when it pays attention only to one thing. When we emphasize one thing, another brother emphasizes another thing, and someone else emphasizes yet another—this means development for the whole church. But as soon as we place ourselves before the church, the church is finished. I can acknowledge that you are better than many brothers, but you can never equal all the brothers. It is the Lord Himself who equals the whole church, not us. Even the youngest brother may notice what we fail to notice. The good point of some brothers is love, but this is not true of all the brothers. If we see this, the church can grow in a balanced way.

(12) If a certain church wants to observe "Christmas," those who serve God faithfully have to go another way; there is absolutely no "Christmas" or "Easter" in the Bible. If the church wants to observe these occasions, we can immediately conclude that the church is not going on properly. There are many other things that are not found in the Bible such as the idols of Roman Catholicism. If we yield to these, trouble will definitely come.

Several Basic Principles

In summarizing the above points, there are several basic principles. First, the church must stand on the positive side of whatever is in the Bible and forbear the negative side. If some are weak and unable to come up to what is in the Bible, the church needs to forbear.

Second, certain truths in the Bible have two sides, as we have already spoken of concerning the doctrine of holiness. Thus, the church must also have both sides. Having only one side will bring forth a sect.

Third, by all means the church must reject what is not in the Bible. Otherwise, those who follow the Lord faithfully will leave when they see the church practicing what is not in the Bible.

At any rate, we must stand on the positive side of what is in the Bible. Whenever the Bible allows both sides, we must stand on both sides. However, we must reject whatever is not in the Bible.

Fourth, we should allow people the freedom for whatever the Bible allows people freedom for, such as observing the Lord's Day or the Sabbath day. This does not mean that the Bible does not believe in the Lord's Day, but that the weak ones still believe in the Sabbath day. They are still Jews. The Bible absolutely approves of eating meat. But if some are in favor of being vegetarian, the church must allow them to be vegetarian. This keeping of the Sabbath day does not refer to the Seventh-day Adventists. Seventh-day Adventism involves the matter of the law; it is a whole system. This is entirely contrary to the book of Galatians, and it is a heresy not found in the Bible.

The church that includes all of God's children can be counted as the true church. If we have some special doctrine or some special emphasis, if we accept certain kinds of teaching at the expense of the rest of the children of God, we cannot be considered as the church. We cannot be the church without inclusiveness. With inclusiveness we will begin to see that we can be brothers and sisters to all of the children of God. We can be with anyone who loves the Lord. The leading brothers, therefore, must grow before the Lord. They must touch the highest and the most perfect. Let me repeat: If we have not attained to the highest, our heart should be big enough so that we do not hinder our brothers under any circumstance. If we cannot attain or climb up and do not allow others to go on, we are a sect, not a church.

We do not become a church just by putting up the name of the local church. We become a church only when there is spiritual inclusiveness that includes all of the children of God. If the church includes rather than excludes God's children, the church will not be responsible for brothers who desire to go another way, because it is they who are creating the division, not the church. Therefore, we must be broken to pieces! We must be dug deeply! We cannot consider ourselves the measuring stick of the church; we are too short. God has a work for every brother and sister, and He has committed something to each one of them. When everyone can be placed, there is the church. The church, therefore, must be inclusive, not exclusive.

Everyone Serving

Whether or not a church can stand in the position of the church also depends upon whether she gives all the brothers and sisters the opportunity to work, that is, whether she gives all the brothers and sisters the opportunity to serve God. We must heed one thing: When a believer receives the life of God, he has the disposition to serve God; his nature wants to serve God. If we do not give him the opportunity to serve God, there will be a breakdown, and he will become sectarian. His new nature wants to serve, but if he cannot serve among us, he will find another place to serve. Many sects originate from the desire to work. Many people want to serve God, but because they have no way to get through, they seek another way and become a sect.

The teachings in the Bible are very clear on this matter. There are three portions in the Scripture that show us that the Body of Christ has a special relationship with service. Romans 12:4-5 says, "For just as in one body we have many members, and all the members do not have the same function, so we who are many are one body in Christ, and individually members one of another." These two verses say that we are one body and individually we are members. Verses 6 through 8 say, "And having gifts that differ according to the grace given to us, whether prophecy,...or service,... or he who teaches,...or he who exhorts...." In other words, the church is the Body of Christ. The church, like a body, includes many members. In fact, it includes every member. As a member, we must give each one work to do; we must give each one the opportunity to develop his functions. Paul showed us that no matter what kind of gift we have, we should only function to the extent that our gift allows. We should never do over and above the degree of our faith; we must leave room for other brothers to function. If we do all the work, other brothers will have nothing to do. If we take over all the tasks, other brothers will have no tasks to tackle. If we preach all the messages, other brothers will have nothing to preach.

Therefore, it is better for one person to take one portion in the church, not for one person to take two, and even more. It is better not to do everything. A portion must be assigned to every brother. Every brother and sister must be given the opportunity to serve God just as we have the opportunity to serve God.

First Corinthians 12:27 says, "Now you are the body of Christ, and members individually." Following this it says, "And God has placed some in the church: first apostles, second prophets, third teachers; then works of power, then gifts of healing, helps, administrations, various kinds of tongues" (v. 28). It is wonderful that Paul asks in the next verse, "Are all apostles? Are all prophets? Are all teachers? Do all have works of power?" (v. 29). Are all apostles? God is asking here. Is it true that all are apostles? Because there are prophets who want to occupy God's whole church, teachers who want to occupy God's whole church, and workers of miracles who want to occupy God's whole church, the Lord asks, "Are all prophets? Are all teachers? Do all have works of power?" Even if everyone in the whole church does works of power, that is still not the church. Even if everyone in the church is a prophet or a teacher, that is still not the church. Do all receive the gift of healing? Indeed, there are groups who specialize only in healing. But even if every one of us can heal, we are still not the church. Do all speak in tongues and interpret? Even if every one of us speaks in tongues and interprets, it is still not the church. "Are all...?" means in the Lord's mind "not all," for there should be apostles, teachers, those who help others, those who administrate, etc. When all these various types of functions are put together, then there is the church.

We are perplexed that there are many brothers who prefer only one kind of work. Some brothers simply think that the work they have is the most important. If every brother is a healing brother (and there are such so-called "churches" in America), then the apostles, prophets, and teachers are all useless. Therefore, the places that bear the responsibility of the church must let those who are prophets have the opportunity to prophesy, those who are teachers the opportunity to teach, those who have the gift of healing the opportunity to heal, those who speak in tongues the opportunity to speak in tongues, and those who administrate the opportunity to administrate. As far as the work is concerned, the church should not restrict any brother or sister. This is the church. Otherwise, it is a sect, not the church. If we do not give the brothers and sisters an opportunity to serve, they will seek another way.

If the young brothers have a mixture of the flesh, we can only exercise authority to deal with them. The Lord has absolutely no intention that those with one talent should bury their talent. In the Lord's sight, the greatest gift is but five talents and the least is one talent. If the church would put all the one talents into use, it would make up for several of the five talents. If only a few of us are working, the church cannot be strong. This does not mean that the one-talented members who have just recently believed in the Lord will not have some fleshly acts. In many respects we must make them listen and obey; nevertheless, we still have to use them. In dealing with the flesh, we should never deal with the gift. All the brothers who are workers, those who are leaders in the churches, must let every brother have the opportunity to serve. The gifts recorded in Romans 12 are more complicated than those in 1 Corinthians. Prophesying, serving, teaching, exhorting, and giving are all included. When all those of one talent have the opportunity to manifest their gifts, sects cannot appear.

Ephesians 4 has similar words. Verses 11 and 12 say, "And He Himself gave some as apostles and some as prophets and some as evangelists and some as shepherds and teachers, for the perfecting of the saints unto the work of the ministry, unto the building up of the Body of Christ." These verses also show us that the gifts are not the same. Verse 16 says, "Out from whom all the Body, being joined together and being knit together through every joint of the rich supply and through the operation in the measure of each one part, causes the growth of the Body unto the building up of itself in love." God's thought here is that the Body of Christ can be built up only when all the members function. If all the brothers and sisters are not serving, the Body of Christ cannot be built up. The leading brothers in every place must remember that if they are busy while the brothers and sisters are not, then they are failing greatly. We should never think that because we are doing so much that this is good enough. If we can lead other brothers and sisters to work, let me tell you, this will please the Lord. It will please the Lord more if we lead the other brothers and sisters to work more than us.

This is really a matter of how you view yourself. If you think that you can build up the Body of Christ by doing well on your own, then you will simply go on as before. But if you have the vision, you will see that the affairs of the church cannot be managed by yourself alone. At the most, you are but one member of the church. Every member in the Body of Christ has his own work. If you bring each one into the work, then you have touched what is called the Body of Christ. You must see that you cannot replace the brothers and sisters. You absolutely cannot work in their place. No matter how perfect you are, how good you are in your work, or how great are your gifts, you are still not the church if you cannot bring the brothers and sisters into the work. Are all hands? A thousand hands or a hundred hands are a monster, not the body.

I would also go one step further and ask, Is there only one hand? We cannot say that only we can do a certain type of work. We must see that the Body of Christ includes much more than us alone. Everyone can receive grace directly from the Head, not necessarily through us. The Lord's grace always amazes me. How great is His grace! Since the Lord is gracious, He can cause others to receive grace apart from me; He can cause them to receive the blessing of God without passing through me. In the church the Lord can raise up all kinds of workers. We have to bring all the brothers and sisters into the work. We must not make them be the same as us. If only a few brothers are serving in a certain place and the rest of the brothers and sisters cannot work, this is just about the same as the one-man service of the denominations. As one-man service is abominable before God, so is the service of only a few people. The service of the whole Body is what pleases God. God says that everyone must serve. When we bring everyone into the work, we will see that this is the church. This is the content of the church.

Not Having the Thought of a System

Finally, we absolutely must not cherish any thought of having a system. We should not think for any reason that the truth and gospel of God only issue forth from our midst. Our intention is only to meet the people that God uses in every locality. We do not necessarily go to many places to lead others, because God has His own leading in every place. We just go to seek fellowship. We should never take the attitude that we are going to a certain locality to be a pastor. We should not form ourselves into a system. When I go to many places, I am going to seek fellowship. In addition to Elijah, there were also many prophets. There could be several thousand Elijahs in the same place standing on the same ground. They are our brothers, and they also see that we are their brothers.

Suppose a group of brothers has been communicating with each other in a certain locality and we begin in the same place and do not communicate with them. This clearly proves that we do not know the church. Suppose fifty brothers are standing on the ground of the church in a certain locality, and later, another fifty brothers in the same place become enlightened and clearly see the ground of the church. It is certain that these brothers will be together with the first group of brothers. By keeping the ground of locality, the problem of forming a system will not arise. When we are in a locality, we are not there for the establishment of a church of "our" system. Rather, we are for the establishment of the church in that locality. When we are in Chungking, we are the church in Chungking; when we are in Tsingtao, we are the church in Tsingtao. We are not the church of a certain system. We make a great mistake once we become the church of a certain system. Once we have the thought of forming a system, we immediately become a sect.

I would like to use Sian as an example. This is not a

matter of name or of an organization. When the two meetings in Sian were combined, there was difficulty over who would become the leading ones, who would take the responsibility. In group A there were three leading brothers, and in group B there were also three leading brothers. Who would be the leading brothers? Leading ones are not determined by the length of time in the work of God, but by the measure of spiritual experience. The meeting of group A had a history of twenty years, and the meeting of group B had a history of only five months. But the experience of the leading brothers in group A was limited before the Lord, while the experience of the leading brothers in group B was of many years before the Lord. According to the world, when two groups blend together with one having met for twenty years and the other having met for only five months, the ones who take the lead should be those in the more established group. But God's Word does not say this. The leading ones must be those who have a longer history before the Lord, not those who have a longer history of meetings. Therefore, when the two meetings were combined, the leading brothers in group A should have let the leading brothers in group B take the lead. Being a leading brother is not determined by the qualification of a longer history of meetings. The position of the church is based upon time, but the standing of the leading brothers is not determined by the church in which they have been taking the lead. It all depends upon the amount of spiritual experience they have before the Lord.

Seeking the Brothers

Today in Shanghai we must pay considerable attention to this matter. Certain brothers and sisters want to leave the denominations. If they have really seen that locality is the ground fixed by the Bible, they should not establish another meeting under any circumstances. For example, when I left the denominations, I did not think of myself as being the first who left the denominations. In my heart I hoped to meet others who had similarly left the denominations. If I were to leave the denominations in Shanghai, I definitely would go around to seek and inquire whether or not other brothers had also left the denominations. When I was about to leave the denominations thirty years ago in Foochow, I went around Foochow looking for brothers who had already left the denominations. Leaving the denominations did not make me the most wonderful Christian in the whole world. My first thought when I left was to seek brothers. Loving the brothers is part of our nature, and seeking the brothers is also part of our nature. We should be very happy to be together with those who seek the Lord with a pure heart.

Some brothers say that they have left the denominations, but they have more of an intention to set up a church than to leave the denominations. Therefore, they do not seek those who have already left the denominations. The aim of many is to establish their own church. Therefore, they do not feel the preciousness of other brothers who have also left the denominations. Those who truly have left will consider all the brothers who have also left as being lovable and precious. Thus, there are two kinds of people leaving the denominations: The first are those who truly leave the denominations; they seek to be with those who serve the Lord with a pure heart. The others are those who leave the denominations because they want to set up their own church. We can say this about those in Shanghai and also in Tsingtao, Peking, and even in the Northwest. In Shanghai it seems that we have been earlier than others. Today they do not seek us, but we have to seek them. They may have the problem of being in a system, but we should not have this problem. If we go today to Pingliang, Tiensui, or Dihua, we must be careful. The first thing we should do is not to set up a church but to seek the brothers.

If the first thing we do when we arrive at a new place is set up a church, we are committing the same mistake as some of the brothers whom we just mentioned in Shanghai. There is probably a group of brothers whose ground is not wrong and who are going in the right direction. We should not say that they are unfamiliar with the Bible. They are brothers whose ground is not wrong. At any rate, we have to seek the brothers until we are certain there is no one before we may have a new start. Often we can only join others; we cannot have a new start. Under no circumstances should we feel that joining others is shameful, but that setting up a church is glorious. If this is our thought, we can only blame ourselves that we were not born before the apostles. Many people like to set up churches. This is not a sign that they are spiritual but that they are fleshly.

Some young brothers who have just come out of the denominations may be able to lead others. Perhaps a brother was received last Saturday. He may have experienced much discipline in the Lord's hand. Once we have received him, we may have to listen to him on many matters because his personal maturity is not related to his denomination. Anyone who has real spiritual experience must be put in the right place. I hope that the Lord will set His way more and more clearly before the brothers and sisters so that all who truly love the Lord may walk therein.

CHAPTER FOUR

THE UNITY OF THE CHURCH

(A talk to the brothers and sisters in Shanghai on March 6, 1951, published in *The Open Door*, dated April 15, 1951.)

The most important, visible problem of recent days is perhaps the unity of the church. Today we must see the way of unity and how to walk in unity.

According to my knowledge, there are four kinds of unity. From among these four different kinds of unity, we must seek one in which to walk as the children of God. We must be clear which one is in accordance with God's will, which one is scriptural, which one is the proper way for the church, and which one we must take. We must learn to reject the rest. When we see one that is of God, we must reject the ones that are not of God.

What are these four ways? First, there is the unity of Roman Catholicism; second, "spiritual" unity; third, the unity of the church in the locality; and fourth, the unity of the independent congregations. Let us consider these one by one.

The Unity of Roman Catholicism

The Churches during the Apostles' Time Being Local

During the apostles' time, the churches were separated according to localities. I think this matter is very clear. The church in Rome, the church in Corinth, the church in Ephesus, the church in Philippi, the church in Laodicea, and the church in Colossae were all separated according to locality. The church in every locality had its own independent administration. Therefore, in the Bible, Acts 14:23 tells us "they had appointed elders for them in every church," and Titus 1:5 tells us that elders were appointed "in every city." The elders are for the church and the church is in a city. Thus, the elders are for the church in a city. The church takes the city as the unit; otherwise, elders in a city would take care of several churches or elders in a church would take care of several cities. The boundary of a city, therefore, equals the boundary of the church, and the boundary of the church equals the boundary of the elders' administration. This is very clear.

The churches in the early days were not formed into a larger, united church. During the apostles' time, the Scriptures acknowledge the existence of "churches" on this earth, but does not unite these churches into "one church." There were "churches," but not a uniting together as one church in the singular number. This is the reason Paul writes to the Corinthians: "Neither the churches of God" (1 Cor. 11:16). Today when God's children speak about the church, they always speak of the "church of God," not about the "churches of God." In our concept, we always consolidate the churches into one church; therefore, we speak of "the church" rather than "the churches." But in the minds of the apostles, there were individual churches; therefore, they spoke of "the churches of God." The apostles did not unite the churches on earth into one church; otherwise, this phrase "the churches of God" would not have existed. Remember that 1 Corinthians 11 and 14 always speak of "the churches," which means that the churches of God on earth are local. They did not combine all the churches of God on earth into *one* church. This was the situation during the time of the apostles.

The History of Change

After the apostles, the church began to change. The churches in big cities spontaneously began to become powerful. A big city naturally had a greater population; thus, the churches in larger cities became more powerful than churches in small cities or villages. The churches in big cities were inclined to absorb churches in smaller cities and villages so that they became satellites. The big cities became centers, while the smaller cities became accessories around them. As a result, there were changes not only in the organization but also in the administration of the church. Originally, there were several elders in a church. The churches in villages or in small cities also had their own elders. After the apostles passed away, however, a group of people in the early church advocated the doctrine that the authority of the apostles had been committed to the elders or bishops who represented the apostles. This was done out of respect for the apostles. Because they honored the first group of apostles, they were reluctant to designate anyone else as an apostle. They dared not use the title *apostle*.

Later, they appointed *one* from among many elders in a big city to be the bishop. Originally, elders were all bishops (overseers); each one was a bishop. The term *elder* refers to the person himself, and *bishop* refers to his office. But gradually, among the many elders, one was chosen to be a bishop, who became not only the head of the elders in a locality but also the head of the elders in the satellite churches.

This is how the changes came about: First, the church in a big city made all the churches in the small cities and villages its satellites. Later, a head elder was designated out of the big church, who naturally became the head elder of the satellite churches. He was called the bishop. This is a title found in the Bible, but the function now associated with it was not the same as what is in the Bible. In the Bible the elders are bishops. Paul called the elders in Ephesus together and said, "Take heed to yourselves and to all the flock, among whom the Holy Spirit has placed you as overseers [bishops]" (Acts 20:17, 28). The bishops in the Bible were plural; the elders were also plural. But today *one* is picked from among many elders to become the bishop. Only one is bishop while the rest are elders, not bishops. The elders no longer have the authority of a bishop. Smaller localities were united together and given over to the rule of this one bishop. One person was made to rule over many churches, and the matter of regions arose.

This development did not stop at just this level. During this same time the Roman Empire conquered the whole world. Among the many churches, the church in the city of Rome became very big. The city was not only large but also the capital. People throughout the whole world came to Rome to see Caesar. At first a bishop ruled over many places, which resulted in a regional church. As the city of Rome became prominent, it began to claim, "We are the capital, and Caesar lives in our midst." Consequently, the bishop in the church of Rome not only ruled over the elders of the church in Rome but also over the elders in the region surrounding Rome. He not only became the head of the elders within the entire empire but also, more particularly, the head of the bishops of the various regions. This was the pope, the product of an order of ascending rank in the form of a hierarchy. Today the meaning of *bishop* in various denominations is "overseer." The head of all such overseers is the pope. The reason everyone is ambitious to be the bishop of Rome is that once one becomes the bishop in Rome, he is spontaneously the bishop of the whole world and the head of all the elders in the world. Once one becomes the bishop in Rome, he immediately becomes the pope, and he represents Christ. This trend continued until its development became fully complete in the fourth century. By that time, "the churches" as recorded in the Bible no longer existed; they were now "one church." The churches in the whole world became one church. From that day on, "the churches of God" as mentioned in the Bible (1 Cor. 11:16) no longer existed and no longer were mentioned. "The churches of the saints," as mentioned in 1 Corinthians 14:33, also no longer were heard of, no longer were mentioned, and no longer existed. They all became part of the one church of Rome, and all the churches throughout the world became branches of Rome. There were no longer churches associated with just localities.

Was there a scriptural basis for this development? Supposedly, the scriptural basis was the fact that the children of God should be one. Since the Lord has only one church on this earth, they thought that they should be united as "one church." However, they forgot that the Bible speaks of "the churches."

No One Daring to Break the "Unity"

We must take notice of one condition that prevailed after the Roman Catholic Church came into being. We know how the Roman Church was filled with heresy, idols, filthiness, and sins. Why did no brothers or sisters in the church stand up to deal with the situation for eleven hundred years? Could it be that no brothers or sisters had seen the heresies? Could it be that they had not seen the idols? Could it be that they had not seen the filthy sins?

In the eleven hundred years following the fourth century, there were definitely some who saw the heresies, idols, and filthy sins, but not one dared to deal with them! They feared that once they dealt with these things, they would immediately break the "unity." "The church is one," they said. "If we begin to deal with the idols, the church will be divided." They felt that the sin of worshipping idols was great, but the sin of ruining the unity was even greater. Therefore, even though they rejected the worship of idols themselves, they did not speak out. They feared that speaking out might ruin the unity. They knew of the heresies and they knew of the idols; moreover, they hated the heresies and they hated the idols. But even more, they hated to destroy the unity. Therefore, they simply avoided the heresies and idols; they dared not evoke any word, message, or action that might ruin the unity. For a period of one thousand one hundred years no one made any move; they continued to *keep* the unity of the church.

At the time of the Reformation, Martin Luther had no thought of forming another church. He thought that doing such a thing would be a serious sin. Therefore, at the beginning his thought was to improve the Roman Catholic Church; the idea of forming another church was not in his mind. It was the inevitable force of history that brought about the formation of another church. Luther only wanted to improve the Roman Catholic Church; he had no intention of forming a new church.

Here we see one thing: The Roman Catholic Church believes in the unity of the church throughout the world. It believes that only one church should exist in the whole world. That is the reason, during the long history of Rome, that the children of God basically forgot that the "churches" were plural in the Bible. They only wanted the church in the singular. Even when Luther arose, he only saw a united church on the earth. He did not see that God has churches in the Bible. Thus, the unity that was upheld is something manifested in one church—the international, worldwide, universal church. Regardless of where this church stands, it is always the Church of Rome. In Shanghai it is the Church of Rome; in Moscow it is the Church of Rome; in London it is the Church of Rome; in Berlin it is also the Church of Rome. Wherever it is, it is always the Church of Rome. *It* does not call itself the Church of Rome; its proper title is the Catholic Church, the Universal Church. We call it the Church of Rome because we know it comes out of Rome. It calls itself the Catholic Church because it is unified and universal; it includes everyone. In China it is called the Catholic Church. The word *catholic* in Latin simply means universal and general, with no distinction in race or region. No matter where it is, it is always one—one in England, one in Japan, and one in Russia. As long as it comes out of Rome, it is called the Catholic Church. As a result, there is only "one church" on earth.

We must study the Scriptures carefully and accurately before God to ascertain whether or not the church on earth is one church. If it is only one church, we must say that the local church is wrong, and even the many denominations in Protestantism must also confess that they are wrong. If there is but one church, we all have to go back to Rome; if we do not, we are wrong. Therefore, we must study the Scriptures to see whether or not we are wrong.

I know there are some Protestant friends who have said that the church on earth is one and that our churches in different localities are wrong. According to them, the church is always one. Please note that their word condemns them. If the church is one, there is no reason for any of their denominations to exist. If the church is one, then regardless of where it is, it must be the Church of Rome. According to numbers, the Church of Rome is the largest, according to history, it is the oldest church, and according to organization, it is one. If there should be only one church, that is, if the church of God or the church of Christ should be singular, then this would be the scriptural way. We should all return to Rome. However, the Bible does not teach this.

In the last century, John H. Newman, a contemporary of J. N. Darby, was a famous English clergyman. He was not only pious, but he had an excellent mind and wrote many books. He was considered one of the most famous persons in the Anglican Church. The hymn "Lead, Kindly Light" was composed by him. He believed that there was only one church in the world, so he started a movement in the Anglican Church to return to Rome. Of course, he was unsuccessful, because Revelation 2 and 3 clearly show that Sardis cannot go back to Thyatira. He thought that it was logical to leave the Anglican Church and join the Roman Church since there was only one church. After being received as a member of the Roman Church, he was promoted to the position of cardinal over England. A cardinal is next in rank only to the pope. He was not only a bishop but a cardinal. There was only one cardinal in England; he was the archbishop of a large region. When a pope passes away, the new pope is chosen from among the scores of cardinals. Many people have expressed regret for Newman, but in reading his books, I feel that his beginning was consistent with his end. I do not say that he was right, but his behavior matched his doctrine. He believed in only one church; therefore, he went back to Rome. One should not believe in one church and yet remain in the denominations. One should not confess that the church is one and be a pastor in the Anglican Church or an elder in the Presbyterian Church. Newman was thoroughly consistent and uncontradicting. His end harmonized with his beginning. In this regard many people in the denominations cannot compare with him.

The Bible Saying, "the Churches of God"

Does the Bible ever say that there is only one church on the earth? No! The Bible shows us that God establishes *churches* on the earth, that is, *one church in each locality.* Here is an important matter which we must notice before God: In the Bible, God has never united the churches in the many localities together as one church.

Do we have proof of this? Yes! We will look at this matter from three directions. First, after the Romans defeated the

Jewish nation, Judea was changed from a nation into a province of Rome. Many churches, each in one locality, existed in the region, the province, of Judea. When the Bible speaks of the churches of Judea, it does not say the church in Judea, but "the churches" in Judea (1 Thes. 2:14). Have we ever seen the importance of the word *churches?* Although all the churches existed in one province, there was not a provincial church. If there was a provincial church, it would have been recorded as the church in Judea, not as the churches in Judea. Since the Bible speaks of them as the churches in Judea, it means that there were many individual churches, not the uniting together of many as the one church of Judea. There was no such thing as a united church.

Second, we can consider Galatia, which is not a city, but like Judea is a province. When the Bible speaks of Galatia, it never says "the church" in Galatia, but "the churches of Galatia" (1 Cor. 16:1), not *church* in the singular, but *churches* in the plural. This shows us that several churches were not joined together in Galatia to form one church. They were still churches.

Third, during that time the largest province was Asia. We can see that all the important churches were in Asia: Ephesus was in Asia, Colossae was in Asia, and Laodicea was in Asia. We should not consider that Laodicea was not so good because the Bible did not give it a good report in Revelation. In fact, Laodicea was very good in the beginning, and it was a very large place. Many churches existed in Asia (1 Cor. 16:19), but they were not united together as the church in Asia; rather, Revelation 1:4 speaks of "the seven churches which are in Asia." Therefore, there is not a united church in the Bible. The churches in a province did not unite, and the churches in the whole world did not unite. The Bible never indicates that the churches in a province should unite as one church, that the churches in a country should unite as one church, or that the churches on a continent should unite as one church. There is no such church in the Bible. There is no such indication that the churches in the whole world should unite as one church. Acts never speaks of such a thing.

Furthermore, what does Paul say when he speaks of

the church in the Epistles? For example, in 1 Corinthians he speaks of "the churches of God" (11:16) and of "all the churches of the saints" (14:33), that is, he speaks of not one church, but many churches. The church composed of all the saints is not the church, but the *churches* of the saints. Three or four brothers and sisters become a church here, and three or four brothers become a church there. They are the churches of the saints. The Bible does not use the phrase *the church of God* when it refers to the churches on earth; it does not use the phrase *the church of the saints*. The Bible clearly speaks of the *churches* of God and the *churches* of the saints. It is evident that God has no thought of uniting all the churches into one church.

In order for God to do something, He must first accomplish two works: The doctrine must be preached, and the apostles must work it out. There is no doctrine of uniting the churches. I have studied the Bible many times, but I have never seen a doctrine in it that indicates that there is only one church on earth. Neither do the apostles work toward such a thing. The Lord wanted the apostles to be completely obedient; He would not let them have their own opinions and act by themselves. Everything done by the apostles was done in obedience to the Lord; therefore, they were qualified to be apostles. If they had acted by themselves and by their own opinions, God would not have acknowledged their work as His work because a distance would have existed between them. God demanded that they obey completely and be thoroughly consecrated. Then God acknowledged what they did as His own work. The apostles did not unite the churches on earth into one church. We do not have such an apostolic pattern, nor do we have such a scriptural teaching.

If God intended to unite all the churches on the earth into one big, grand church, why did He not do such a thing through the hands of such men as Peter, James, John, and Paul? Why did He wait three or four hundred years to accomplish this through the pope? I believe in the pattern of Peter and Paul, but not in the pattern of the pope. I believe in the things done by Peter and Paul, but not in the things done by the pope. I believe in the apostles who were absolute to the

Lord, but not in the popes. We absolutely cannot follow them. This is the reason I do not believe in such a thing as the Church of Christ in China. The church is local. There are only "the churches" of Christ in China, not "the Church" of Christ in China. Brothers, do you see the difference? Only the churches in China, not the church in China, should exist. There should be one church in Shanghai, one church in Tientsin. There may well be 8,000 or 9,000 churches throughout the whole of China, but it is absolutely impossible to make them become *one* church in China.

We see one thing here: The Bible contains absolutely no pattern or commandment for combining all the churches on earth into one organized, formal church. On the contrary, all the patterns and all the teachings in the Bible show that the churches are local and plural in number.

If I am a seeker after God, I cannot join the Roman Catholic Church. It is a worldly organization, one in which all the churches in the whole world are combined into one church. In this one church, the pope acts like an emperor, and the cardinals act like princes in each nation. Since they are an organization of the world, we cannot join them. When we speak with the brothers and sisters in different localities about the unity of the church, we must tell them that our unity is not the unity of the Roman Catholic Church. Today on this earth, there is a unity which is the unity of the Roman Catholic Church. This will not do, because it is not of God. According to history, this is something worked out by man; it is not what God wants us to have.

"Spiritual" Unity

There is a second kind of unity today which can be found throughout the world, and it is called "spiritual" unity. What is the definition of this spiritual unity, and from where does it originate?

State Religions

Originally, Roman Catholicism was the state religion of the Roman Empire. The term *state religion* has a very interesting definition: It means the religion of a nation. The nation, the king, or the emperor ordains such a religion for its people. In other words, once a person is born as a subject of a nation, he becomes a member of the religion of that nation. If a person is a Roman citizen, he automatically joins the Roman religion. Either a person has no nationality and therefore has no membership in any nation's religion, or he is born a citizen of a nation and consequently is a member of the religion of that nation. Whether or not he is willing, he must take part in that religion. This is not a matter that is left up to him to decide; it has been decided by the emperor. If he depends upon the nation for his living, he must take part in the nation's religion.

After the Roman Empire accepted Roman Catholicism as the state religion, the membership of the Roman Catholic Church became the same as the population of the Roman Empire. Formerly, the members of the church only equaled the number of those who through repentance had been regenerated and baptized. Now, however, no one needed to join the church per se. As long as one was born in the country and his father was a Roman, he was qualified to become a member of the Roman religion. There was no need for him to experience regeneration. My father is Chinese, and I was born of my father. It is unnecessary for me to be naturalized in order for me to become a Chinese, because I am Chinese by birth. This was the situation in the Roman Catholic Church; once one was born a Roman, he was a member of the Roman Catholic Church. One who was born of the flesh could now become a "child" of God. This completely changed the word in John 1:12-13. It became unnecessary to be born of God or to receive the Lord Jesus. Instead, being born of blood, of the will of the flesh, and of the will of man was all that was necessary. As long as one was a Roman, he was a member of the Roman Catholic Church. This was the Roman Catholic Church.

Protestantism Originally Being a State Religion Also

At the beginning of the Protestant movement, Martin Luther only wanted to reform the Roman Catholic Church; he did not expect to form a new church. The formation of a new church was not due to religious reasons, but to political ones. Because the Roman pope ruled over the whole world, even the emperor was afraid of him. According to the pope, emperors ruled over the human body, while he ruled over the human soul. Even though the pope's body was ruled over by the emperor, the emperor's soul was ruled over by the pope. The Kaiser could have been the greatest imperialist, but he could do nothing against the pope; the pope ruled over him. If the pope closed the door to the heavenly kingdom, no one could enter in, not even a king. In effect, the pope ruled over the whole world. Thus, the kings of all the nations were very afraid of him. They were kings, yet someone ruled over them. They were kings, yet someone above them was their king. The pope was the supreme ruler of the whole world.

When Luther rose up to reform the church, these kings realized that there was a way for them to separate themselves from Rome. They did not want the pope to rule over their souls; they wanted to rule themselves. They wanted a different church, one not ruled over by the pope. In certain things the commandments they gave could be altered by the pope. The pope could just issue another commandment, and the people dared not disobey, because disobedience to the pope meant that their souls would go to hell. Luther rose up and took advantage of this opportunity. He preached justification by faith, that is, the right of every man to go to God. There were many kings and princes who waited for Luther to go ahead and who were willing to support him with force. The pope tried to quell the reformers by force. In response, the kings seized the opportunity to send out armies to battle, and the fighting was fierce. Afterwards, not only was there a separation of doctrine but also a separation from the Roman Catholic Church. What was the result? Those who followed Luther's teaching became part of the Church of Germany in Germany, the Church of Holland in Holland, and the Church of England in England. Originally, the Roman Empire encompassed the whole world. Germany, Holland, and England were smaller kingdoms within it. Now Germany had its own Lutheran Church, Holland had its own Dutch Reformed Church, and England had its own Anglican Church. These were also state churches, only they were smaller than the Roman Church.

Anyone born of British parents becomes a member of the Anglican Church. The moment one comes out of the womb of his mother, he is automatically a member of the Anglican Church. This is the reason behind infant baptism. It is necessary to have an infant registered in the church. Since he is British, he is automatically a member of the Anglican Church. It is unnecessary to believe. It is only a matter of registration. If he is registered, he is a member. One can be born an Englishman and a Christian at the same time. Later, when private churches were raised up, the members had to leave the Anglican Church. Members of these private churches were called "dissenters," which means that they dissented from the state church. They were originally in the state church, but when they wanted to come out they first had to leave the state church in order to join another. If a person wanted to join the Wesleyan Church, he first had to leave the Anglican Church. They were dissenters; otherwise, they would not have come out.

The Doctrine of the Visible and the Invisible Church Produced

At this point a problem arose. Since both the Roman Catholic Church and the Protestant Church were state churches, they naturally contained many unsaved people. A person cannot be saved by birth. If a person could be saved by birth, we would only have to make Christianity the state religion of China and then all the Chinese would be Christians. Becoming a Christian by regeneration would become unnecessary. However, this is impossible. Being born is one thing, but being born again is quite another. As a result of such a practice, all the state churches were filled with unsaved people. Thank God, there were also many saved ones. But the unsaved people, in spite of their education and background, were still unsaved.

There then is a problem: Is the Anglican Church the church? If it is the church, how could there be so many unsaved people in it? Surely this is quite strange! In this church there are quite a number of unbelievers. How could this be? Consequently, a certain doctrine of the church emerged. According to this doctrine, there are two kinds of churches: *visible and invisible,* that is, *a church with a form and another church without a form.* In this doctrine the church spoken of in the Scriptures was regarded as invisible and spiritual, but the church on the earth was regarded as visible and with a form. In the visible church there could be false Christians, but in the spiritual church everyone was genuine. Brothers, we must know that all doctrines have an origin. The doctrine of the spiritual church, that is, the doctrine of a visible and an invisible church, was brought in just as we have mentioned. Since man brought in so many false believers, the visible church, of course, became untrustworthy. Since all the British people fell into one net, there had to be both "good fish" and "bad fish." This is wrong. The Scriptures teach that the church is the Body of Christ and Christ is the Head of the church; thus, only believers can be the church. How can there be unbelievers in the church? Since so many unbelievers filled the church, what else could be done except to produce a doctrine about two kinds of churches, a visible one which is unreliable and an invisible one which is real? It was inevitable that this kind of doctrine would be produced. It was essential to justify their existence; otherwise, it was impossible for them to go on. Brothers, do you see the point? It is by necessity that this kind of doctrine was produced. The visible church became too loose; anything could be found in her. As a result, such a doctrine was compelled to be produced.

Supporters of this doctrine quoted the Scripture where it says that Satan sowed tares after the Lord sowed the seed. It says that we should not remove the tares, but "let both grow together" (Matt. 13:24, 30). These ones said that the invisible and spiritual church consists of those who are born again, among whom not one is false. But in the visible church there are tares, which should not be removed. Many brothers and sisters reading this passage thought that this was right, that there was a difference between the visible and the invisible church. They did not realize that such evil can never be covered up by the doctrine of the visible and invisible churches. These ones made the church too inclusive. The Lord Jesus was speaking about the wheat and the tares growing together in the world (Matt. 13:38), not in the church! Since the church was expanded to be as large as the world, naturally tares were included in the church. Consequently, the only way to explain the church was to say that there is a church with form and a church without form. It is true that these ones acknowledged that the Anglican Church is too big. But there is another church, the church in the Bible, which only consists of spiritual and regenerated persons.

What was the condition of the churches on earth in Revelation 2 and 3? They were the seven golden lampstands. What is a golden lampstand? It is a place where light shines forth. When He was on earth, the Lord Jesus said, "Let your light shine before men." What is the use if the light shines, but men cannot see it (Matt. 5:16)? Tonight, we can be here because there is visible light. What could we do if it were invisible? An invisible light is a joke, a big joke. How can there be an invisible light? Furthermore, if light is visible, it must have a form; it cannot be without form. A light without form is a lie. The church on the earth must be seen by men. The Bible has no thought of the church being an invisible light. But today, the church is spoken of not in relation to putting a lamp under a bushel, but of shining forth invisible light from a lampstand! The word that the Lord Jesus spoke to us is clear enough. He said, "You are the light of the world. It is impossible for a city situated upon a mountain to be hidden" (Matt. 5:14). This is visible, not invisible. The Lord wants us to be manifested on the earth and seen of men.

We must see, therefore, that what is called the visible church is actually the world. Because some insist on calling it a church, they explain that there is another church within this outward church. However, the church spoken of in God's Word is one that comes out of the world and is separated from the world. Since this is so, we only can acknowledge the existence of a spiritual church, not an outward church.

The problem today is that there are many brothers and sisters who think that the unity among Christians is a "spiritual" unity. According to this spiritual unity, there are some people in the church who are spiritual and some who are not. Thus, in every church there is an outward aspect and a spiritual aspect. With spiritual unity, a group of spiritual brothers can have fellowship with another group of spiritual brothers, and they can all be one with each other. I want to point out that the reason there is a need for this kind of spiritual unity is that there are some who are of the world. If everyone is brought forth by the word of God, the question of spiritual unity would never need to arise.

This matter is very important because it touches a basic problem. If you ask someone how many are unsaved in his denomination, he would probably say about half of them. Several denominations may tell you that they would be very happy if one in ten is saved. These denominations are not much different from the state church. They are like an onion which has many layers that can be peeled off. What they mean is that the nine outside layers mean nothing; only the center counts. Undoubtedly, the principle of the denominations is still the principle of the state church because many in their midst do not belong to the Lord. For this reason their fellowship must, by necessity, be limited to spiritual ones, not to the whole church. If the whole church were to fellowship together, many unbelievers would be involved. In order to have spiritual fellowship, the whole church cannot be included. But the Bible includes the whole church as the boundary of fellowship. Because the condition of the church is murky and the boundary of the church is ill-defined, there is the need of "spiritual" fellowship.

Today many kinds of peculiar churches exist in the world because many non-Christians were brought into them. Since many unbelievers and false Christians are in the "church," Christians in these churches have to maintain an invisible fellowship; all their fellowship is invisible. They say that they have fellowship of the heart, that their hearts are joined to each other. Let me say this: The very need for this kind of fellowship is a mistake. We must understand and see through this. This need for "spiritual" unity exists only because the position is wrong. If we stand in the right position, we are already one. If the church is proper, the invisible would become visible, and there would be no need for invisible fellowship. The Lord said that the church is a lampstand, but they say that the light it sheds is only an invisible light. This is strange. This kind of spiritual fellowship and spiritual unity was produced by mixing unbelievers in the church.

The Producing of Many Denominations

This view creates two problems: we have just seen the problem from the viewpoint of the state church; now we must see it from the viewpoint of the dissenters, many of whom did not approve of the state church. They not only disapproved but also stood up to oppose the errors of the state church. Such were the Baptists, the Presbyterians, and the Wesleyans. The Wesleyans thought that preaching could be done everywhere. As dissenters, they rose up and formed churches to maintain the truth based upon their dissent. Thus, the Baptist Church, the Presbyterian Church, the Wesleyan Church, the Quaker Church, and later several thousand groups, arose. In England they were called the dissenters. In the Russian Empire, the state church was called the Russian Orthodox Church, and the rest were called sects. All these brothers rose up for the truth. This is a good point! We thank God for this. Regrettably, however, they tried to maintain God's truth by setting up new churches, thus causing the church of God to be divided into several thousand parts.

Later, the situation gradually changed. In the first generation of their existence both sides argued considerably. For example, Wesley argued fiercely with the Church of England. In the third and fourth generations, however, the arguing subsided, and there was not much difference between them. Formerly, they would not greet one another and communicate with each other, but today they even pray together. For example, the United Christian Church, which was originally in the Wesleyan Church, demanded that Wesleyans accept the doctrine of divine healing. They argued so terribly over this matter that they later separated. Now in the third generation, they no longer argue. In the beginning the differences were great, but now they are not great. Some of the people in

the United Christian Church, however, believed in the out-
pouring of the Holy Spirit and speaking in tongues. They left
to establish the Pentecostal Church. At first, there were terrible arguments among them, but now it no longer matters.

Today all these churches have been formed. Some formed
the Baptist Church because of baptism, some formed the
Lutheran Church because of Luther, some formed the Meth-
odist Church because of Wesley, and some formed the
Christian and Missionary Alliance because of Simpson. In
the Bible, however, no church was formed based on a certain
doctrine. There is not one instance in the Bible where a
special doctrine warrants the establishment of a church.
According to the apostle Paul, the doctrines which men have
argued most strongly about were not major problems. In
Romans 14 Paul said it is all right for one man to observe this
day while another observes another day. Some may be for one
day, while others may be for another day, while still others
may be for both days (vv. 5-6). These people are weak in the
faith. But they should not be divided by doctrines. Some do
not eat meat because they are weak in the faith, but they feel
it is all right to eat vegetables (v. 2). Paul did not form a vegetarian church, nor did he form a meat-eating church. Some
ate vegetables and some ate meat. Paul said none of these
should pose any problem; we should receive those whom the
Lord has received because God has received them (Rom.
14:3). If he eats vegetables, he is a brother; if he eats meat, he
is still a brother. If he observes this day, he is a brother; if
he observes another day, he is still a brother. There is no
example in the Bible of forming a church according to doctrine.

According to the Bible, how is the church formed? The only
requirement is in Romans 14: "Receive...for God has received
him" (vv. 1, 3). We must receive whomever God receives. We
receive him because God has received him. He has the life of
God. Formerly, he was a sinner, but now he has come to
the Lord. The only question we need to ask is whether or not
he has received the Lord. If he has, any further word is
unnecessary. As to his behavior as a Christian, we should
help him with the teachings of the Bible, but we cannot refuse

him and put him outside the church. Some believe in baptism by sprinkling; they are better than those who do not baptize at all. The Salvation Army does not sprinkle and neither do the Quakers. Some baptize by rubbing drops of water; others baptize by immersion. Philip and the eunuch went down into the water (Acts 8:38), and the Lord Jesus came out of the water (Matt. 3:16). Going down and coming up must mean baptism by immersion. However, some people only immerse their hands in the water, not their bodies. According to the Scriptures, we must be immersed. Today some baptize by rubbing on water. We should not tell them that they belong to the "water-rubbing" church. We cannot establish a church according to doctrine. Regardless of whether baptism is by immersion or by rubbing on water, we can only ask, Have these brothers been received by God? Have these brothers been saved? If they are saved, despite whether or not they have been rubbed with water, they will stand before God. How can we not receive them? If we are going to spend eternity with them, how can we not receive them today? How can we each go our own way because we cannot accept others' shortcomings? This should not be! The Bible shows that the church includes all those whom the Lord has received.

Furthermore, in Romans 14 Paul said, "Now him who is weak in faith receive," not reject. We recognize that this brother is weak, but we must not reject him; rather, we must receive him. Often we err by considering that he can follow us only if his faith is as strong as ours. Instead, we need to see that we must receive those who are weak in the faith. If we reject them, at the most we can shut them out of the church for a few score of years. We cannot shut them out forever. We have no way to excommunicate them; they are our brothers forever. We must realize that to divide the church according to doctrines will not work. Suppose a brother in the church at Sian is a vegetarian. What should we say? We can only ask one question: Has this person been saved? If he has been saved and continues his diet of vegetables, we must allow him to do so. In other words, he has received the same life; there-fore, regardless of his preference, we have to receive him. We must help those who are weak in the faith with the teachings of the Bible, not separate from them by forming another church.

Today, the so-called denominations have been brought forth as the result of division over doctrines. People take a doctrine from the Bible, preach it, and form a denomination around it. Consequently, there is the Pentecostal Church, the Lutheran Church, the Quakers, etc. The Quakers stress a gesture (quaking), the Lutherans a doctrine, the Presbyterians an organization, and the Congregationalists an independent congregation. These are not the work of the Lord but the result of man's ideas which have divided the children of God into so many denominations.

Many think it is good to have denominations because it is convenient. Brothers! if you asked me whether or not I like denominations according to the flesh, I would say, "Yes, I like them, because everything is clear-cut. Those who like to speak in tongues can go to the Tongues Church, those who like independent congregations can go to the Congregational Church, and those who do not like sprinkling can go to the Salvation Army." But the Bible teaches that there should be only one church in each locality. In Corinth there is only one church, in Ephesus there is only one church, and in Shanghai there should be only one church. This way is not convenient because everyone must love all of the brothers! Loving many brothers who are not like us causes much friction and many lessons. You have your proposals, and I have my proposals; you have your ideas, and I have my ideas. It is very convenient for you to have your church and for me to have my church. It is not so convenient for us today; to be together in one church means that we have to love one another. With many difficulties there are many lessons, but with more difficulties, there also is the need for more love for one another. Even though we are unhappy, we still cannot escape. Whether or not we like it, we still must be brothers together. We must overcome the carnal by the spiritual, conquer all differences by love, and cover all difficulties by grace. Otherwise, the church cannot succeed.

Holding Hands over the Fences Not Being Unity

Since people already have the denominations today, what should we do? We have already testified that it is not good for God's children to have denominations and divisions. God's children must not form divisions; rather, God's children must love one another and be together. We have been saying this for thirty years since 1921. Is this word effective? Yes. Although we have met much opposition from the beginning and are still meeting some today, the opposition is getting weaker and weaker. At the beginning they tried to defend the denominations. Today they have become much weaker. Now they have come up with another way, saying, "We want to have a spiritual fellowship." As we have seen, this spiritual fellowship is the result of two factors. The first factor is state churches, in which a small church was found within a large church, a true church within a false church, a church of reality within a church of externality. The second factor is divisions caused by the differences in doctrines. Now some seek a middle road, that is, having "spiritual" fellowship with one another. Let us see if this "spiritual" fellowship is right or wrong.

"Spiritual" fellowship is certainly an improvement upon no fellowship among the denominations. Thank God! The situation in China through these many years has certainly changed, but can "spiritual" fellowship replace the fellowship of the church as ordained in the Bible? What they call "spiritual" fellowship is not real fellowship; they only borrow the term. For example, here we have several cups. God's purpose is that all should be united as one cup, but they have made the mistake of dividing themselves into many cups. "Spiritual" fellowship is for the purpose of strengthening the fellowship in the denominations. In denominationalism I have my cup, you have your cup, and he has his cup. "Spiritual" fellowship is a stretching out of our hands over our cups to hold each others' hand "across the fence." Separation by fences is denominationalism. Holding hands over the fences is "spiritual" fellowship. There is still sectarianism despite a desire for fellowship. If we do not hold hands over the fences, however, we are sectarian and denominational. According to the teaching of the Bible, however, there should be no sects, no denominations. Yet today there are brothers who want to keep the denominations, even though their consciences bother them that there is no fellowship. Consequently, they stretch out their hands over the fence to hold hands on the other side. This is the doctrine of the so-called "spiritual" fellowship today.

Concerning this matter, I feel quite heavy within. Brothers, let me say one word: If denominations are scriptural, we must pay any price to maintain the denominations. If it is God's command, who can nullify it? We must learn to follow God, not man. However, if the denominations are wrong, we must abolish them to the root. We cannot confess that the denominations are wrong on the one hand and encourage them on the other hand. We cannot say that denominations have no standing on the one hand and maintain them on the other hand. Since the denominations have no standing, we have to break them down and abolish them. We cannot covet fellowship on the one hand and have fellowship over fences on the other hand. If we really desire fellowship, we must break down the fences and have fellowship. If we want to serve God and feel that all God's children should have fellowship, we must tear down all the fences to have fellowship. If the fences are right, then we must build fences, not only ten feet high, but ten thousand feet high. We must be thorough and absolute before God. If the denominations are right, we must exert one thousand times the effort. This is proper. If the denominations are wrong, then it is proper for us to tear them down. If we feel that the denominations are wrong, yet want to keep the fences and shake hands over the fences, this is not the principle for serving God. The basic principle for us to serve God is that if we feel the denominations are right, we must support them; if we feel they are wrong, we must break them down. If we want to support the denominations on the one hand and try to break them down on the other, what could we hope to accomplish?

You must come to the place of showing others that their actions are not according to God's will. Speak for yourself. If you feel the denominations are right, you should help them. If you feel the denominations are wrong, then please tear them down. Do not merely pull the fences lower; tear them down completely. If the denominations are right, you must build the fences higher, so that no one can cross over, and so that everyone is clearly divided. This matter must be thorough and absolute. Keeping the denominations on the one hand, and feeling that they are wrong while trying to repair them on the other hand is absolutely not God's way. You know God; you have read the Bible—have you ever seen God wanting men to repair something? This is what is done by those who lack the courage to answer God's demand and listen to God's Word. They are paying half or less than half the price; they are seeking some bargain. They hold out their hand of fellowship while keeping the fences of division. I would like you brothers to see this matter clearly. A basic principle of Christian behavior is that we must pursue every matter thoroughly and absolutely. Then we can solve the problem.

For a clearer understanding, I will give an illustration. The Bible shows that God accepted Abel's offering but not Cain's (Gen. 4:2-7). Cain was a farmer and cultivated the soil. This is what his father did when he was in the Garden of Eden. When his father tilled the soil in the Garden of Eden, he brought the produce of the land and offered it to God. Even though Cain was outside the Garden of Eden because of sin, he tilled the soil as before. He received produce from the land as before, and he offered it to God as before. God not only refused to accept him, but also was displeased with him. Some people ask, "Why?" This is very simple and has but one significance: What man did before he sinned was acceptable to God, but nothing can be worse before God than to do the same thing after man sinned. Suppose that at eight o'clock each evening a child wants his mother to prepare a snack for him before he goes to bed. But one day he causes some trouble, and his mother has to apologize and pay for damages. What would happen if he asked his mother to prepare a snack for him as usual as though nothing had occurred? What would you say? If the child had been crying and was upset over his actions, you might not feel too bad. But if he acts as if nothing has happened, you would feel very bad. If a child is not bothered after making trouble, when he grows up he may even kill people and not be bothered. Cain was just like this. What he had done before, he continued to do in the same way after having sinned. He continued to offer things to God as though nothing had happened. He considered committing sin a small matter; he did not think it was anything serious. Abel was accepted because he acknowledged that he was outside the Garden of Eden. His offering acknowledged that he had sinned and that his present situation was different from what it had been in the past.

We are afraid of frivolous people like Cain; this kind of people cannot serve God. This is a basic principle. They say, "We are in the denominations. The denominations were not formed by us; they were formed by our forefathers. We bear some responsibility in them. We cannot say, 'Good! Let us be united tomorrow.' This is impossible. What about the denominations we are in?" God wants the church to be united, but denominations divide it! When one begins to be conscious that it is wrong to be divided in this way, he must confess that this is wrong before God; he must tear it down. He should say, "O God, although this denomination was not formed by me but by my forefathers, I am sinful as long as I am a part of it. This is not just a personal matter; it involves the whole church of God. This is sin. Today I would ask You to tear it down; today I would declare that there is something wrong in it." This is the right way to act. Suppose I form a denomination and afterwards realize that something is wrong and try to ameliorate it by saying, "Let us have fellowship." I am afraid of this kind of frivolous and light-minded behavior. This is Cain's behavior, not condemning sin after he had sinned but trying to repair the situation instead. This is very unchristian. Brothers, are you clear? Do not think it is all right to not condemn but only attempt to repair it after you have sinned. This is never the expression of God's life!

For example, suppose I offend a brother by speaking many things behind his back. What should I do when I am rebuked by God's light? First, I must go to him and confess my sin: "Brother, I have sinned against you by speaking many things to undermine you behind your back. Please accept my apology." Then it is right for me to express some love to him the next day. What if a man sins against you, steals many things from you, speaks against you, and then behaves as if nothing has happened? He does not confess his sin at all, but turns around to treat you well and to send gifts to you. How would you feel about him? We Christians do have a way of doing things. If we have done something wrong, we cannot change a little without confessing our mistake. It is not right to act this way. This is not the way before God to solve our problems. Such a person should come to you and confess, "Brother, I am wrong. I owe you money, and I owe you other things." He must first confess his sin before he can show his love. This is the principle by which a Christian may be restored.

The principle here is the same. Today it is not just a matter of whether or not the denominations are right. What matters is that if we feel they are right, we must support them, but if we feel they are wrong, we have to tear them down. We should not shake hands over the fence. If we say it is right to have the fence, then we must build it higher. If we feel the fence is wrong, we must tear it down. We should not have "spiritual" fellowship. What they call "spiritual" fellowship means a fellowship that is not thorough enough. Even though the denominations are wrong, some are reluctant to forsake them; they still want to preserve them while at the same time stretching their hand out for a little fellowship with others. If we fall into this category, it is definitely not of God. I do not know if we see this clearly. We must see this thoroughly before we can go out to deal with the situations in each locality. It is not enough for those who formerly closed themselves from others to merely open the window, shake hands over the fence, and think that this is all they need to do. If this fence should exist, I will build it stronger and higher, but if this fence should not exist, I will tear it down. Keeping different denominations and yet having fellowship is self-deception.

Today in China, there are probably three kinds of unity. The first kind is the unity of the Roman Catholic Church. The second kind is the "spiritual unity," which means that although the separating "cups" still exist outwardly, one tells himself that such "cups" do not exist in his heart. This seems strange to me! If the denominations are not important, why should people allow them to exist? If the denominations are not important, why do people react when the denominations are touched? It is quite puzzling. If the denominations are important, we should support them; if they are not, we should tear them down. If fellowship is necessary, let us fellowship and not have the so-called "spiritual" fellowship. This is a really good term, but its usage has been spoiled. It is not really a "spiritual" fellowship but only a "half-way" fellowship! If this matter is made clear, I think the problem of unity can be solved easily.

With this kind of "spiritual" unity there is a great problem: Those who advocate "spiritual" unity give their attention to God's children while neglecting God's command. In other words, they pay attention to the feeling of God's children but forget the feeling of God Himself. A man who supports the denominations is one who knows God very little. But many people dare not support the denominations if they are asked. They feel that the denominations are sin. However, because they have a consideration for many of God's children in the denominations, they are not faithful enough to thoroughly unveil the truth of God to them. They do not show them how the divisions among God's children are against God's will. They are afraid that this will create some kind of partition between them and many of God's children who are in the denominations. If they are asked whether or not they advocate and support the denominations, they would be somewhat bothered because they have studied the Word and received some light. Denominations are condemned before God and rejected by God. Nevertheless, they want to have a "spiritual" unity. This kind of "spiritual" unity or this attitude of shaking hands over the fence is nothing but a method to accommodate, a method to reconcile, and a method of compromise. They dare not utterly uphold the denominations, but they are reluctant to utterly forsake the denominations. Consequently, they allow the denominations to exist and advocate a "spiritual" unity, a "spiritual" fellowship. The real significance of what they call "spiritual" unity is a reluctance to be absolute toward God or to follow His Word. They dare not be absolute toward God for fear of men. The fear of being absolute toward God is today's difficulty. In fact, many advocate "spiritual" fellowship and "spiritual" oneness because they cannot come up to the Lord's demand; they are not absolute toward the Lord. This method is not from the teaching of the Scriptures, but from man's wisdom and fear.

I believe that when we do not stand on the side of God's children to excuse their weaknesses and their failures, but stand on the Lord's side to look at His glory and His holiness, we will see that unity by accommodation is not of the Lord's will and is not scriptural. We must be very clear about this. If we are clear about this, we can solve the problems.

The Unity in the Scriptures

Now we will look at the third kind of unity, that is, the unity in the Scriptures.

The Inherent Unity of the Body

The Scriptures show us that the church is the Body of Christ and that there is only one Body. The Scriptures also show us that God through the Holy Spirit dwells in the church and that the Holy Spirit is one Spirit. Thus, the Scriptures give special attention to the "one Spirit" and the "one Body" (1 Cor. 12:12-13; Eph. 4:4). We also must give our special attention to this.

The church of Christ is the Body of Christ. If we only consider it as the church, we may not feel that it matters whether or not there is some division, thinking that little harm is done even though there is a little division here and a little division there. If we only consider it as God's people, again it may not matter whether or not there is some division here and there. If we only consider it as God's army, it may not matter whether or not there is some division. Finally, if we only consider it as the house of God, it may be all right if it is divided into several houses. But the Word of God also tells us that the church of Christ is the Body of Christ. With a body, division is absolutely impossible. We cannot separate three members here and five members there and another two over there. It is impossible. Everything else in the world can be divided, but not the body. Once the body is divided, it becomes a corpse. Once the church is divided, the world only has the corpse of Christ, not the Body of Christ. It is a serious matter to God when the church is divided. The children of God cannot be divided, just as the body cannot be divided. The church cannot be divided. Yet today, God's children have become insensitive to divisions; they do not consider them as a serious matter. Please remember, a body cannot be divided! The church is the Body of Christ. In nature it is the Body, and one Spirit dwells in it. Therefore, the unity of the church in the Scriptures is the unity of the nature of the Body, which is indivisible.

Today we want to ask one question: Since the Bible shows us that the unity of the church is the unity of the one Holy Spirit dwelling in the one Body, how can it be expressed?

Not One Church, but Seven Golden Lampstands

The Roman Catholic Church tells us that since the Body of Christ is one, we should only organize one church on the earth. We have already seen that this is not the teaching of the Scriptures. The Scriptures do say that the Body of Christ is one, but they never require the church on the earth to become one like the Roman Catholic Church. Otherwise, the word *churches* would be a great mistake and the Scriptures should not contain such a term. We cannot say *churches* and also say *one church*. Since the Scriptures speak of "churches," we know that God has no intention of uniting all the churches on the earth into one church. Furthermore, the apostles in the Bible never organized one church. They established churches in many places, and they established one church in each city. The Holy Spirit did not lead them to establish just one church. One worldwide church is only the opinion of the Roman Catholic Church; the unity of Roman Catholicism is manmade, not scriptural.

Let us look at the Scriptures again. We see the outward appearance of the church on this earth, which might be wrong. By the outward appearance alone, it may not be easy to understand whether the church on the earth should be many churches or one church. The best way is to go before the Lord and see how the Lord looks at the churches on the earth. This cannot be wrong. Thank God! According to the Scriptures, the church in each locality has a representative before the Lord. This is the preciousness of Revelation 1—3, which shows us the "seven churches in Asia." This does not mean that only seven churches existed on this earth but that these seven were representative examples. Revelation 1—3 shows us how the seven churches in Asia were before the Lord in heaven. There were seven golden lampstands placed before Him. Do you see? The churches on earth may be wrong, entirely wrong, but the churches in heaven, the churches before the throne, the churches before the Lord, cannot be wrong. Saying these churches are wrong is blasphemous and terrible!

How were the seven churches in Asia before the Lord? They were *seven golden lampstands.* In other words, for every church on the earth, there is a golden lampstand in heaven. These seven churches were in seven different localities: Ephesus was a locality, Smyrna was a locality, Pergamos was a locality, etc.; there was a total of seven localities. There were seven lampstands in heaven because there were seven churches on earth. It is not God's will to unify the churches on earth into one church. If it were God's will to unify all the churches on earth into one church, then God in heaven would have only one lampstand, not seven. Brothers, this is very clear. We must think, and the Lord causes us to think. If we would just think a little, we would realize that if the Lord has only one church on earth, He would have only one lampstand in heaven. There are seven lampstands, however, and they are seven churches in seven localities. In each locality there is a lampstand. It is obvious to us that God's purpose is not to unify the churches into one church.

The term *lampstand* is very familiar to us; it is also found in the Old Testament. In the Old Testament one lampstand with seven branches was placed before God, signifying that all the Israelites were united as one nation. God did not want the nation of Israel to be divided into two nations. The

division between the nations of Judah and Israel was not
pleasing to God, because before God they were one. Dividing
them into two was sin; therefore, Jeroboam sinned. But in the
New Testament there is not one lampstand with seven
branches, but seven different lampstands. In other words,
God's original thought concerning the church is to have the
respective churches standing before Him independently.

Do you see? There is not one lampstand with seven
branches, but seven lampstands. The Lord was walking in the
midst of these seven lampstands. They were placed there side
by side, and the Lord walked in their midst (Rev. 2:1). If it
were one lampstand with seven branches, the Lord could not
walk in their midst. Therefore, in spiritual reality there are
seven different lampstands before God, not seven lampstands
united as one lampstand. This signifies that God has no
intention of uniting the churches on the earth into one
church. God never had such an intention.

In other words, God's ordained will concerning the nation
of Israel is different from that concerning the church. God's
ordained will concerning Israel is that it might be one nation
on the earth, not two. God appointed only one place for the
whole nation of Israel to worship, which was Jerusalem. The
people of Israel were to go to Jerusalem every year, not to any
other place. They set up Bethel, but this was not pleasing to
God. It was a high place, not God's center. Today God does not
desire that the churches on earth be unified and take Rome
as a center like Jerusalem. Today, there are *seven different*
churches. Therefore, *the unity of the Body of Christ does not
mean that the churches on earth must be formed into one
church.* The Bible does not contradict itself. The Bible shows
us that there is only one Body of Christ. The Bible also shows
us that God does not want the churches to be unified into one
church on the earth. The unity that God desires is not that
the churches should be combined into one big church and
formed into one great unity.

We are studying this matter step by step. We have just
seen how the Bible speaks concerning the Body and the
church. The unity spoken of in the Bible does not refer to the
unity of one big church. To what then does the unity of the

Body, which the Lord desires, refer? It must refer to something else. The unity of Catholicism cannot be applied; it is not of God. This is the first point.

Once There Is a Denomination, There Is a Division

Now we will look at the second point. Our brothers say that we should have a "spiritual" fellowship, a "spiritual" unity. Does the unity of the Body of Christ refer to the "spiritual" unity as advocated by the brothers in the denominations today? It is half "yes" and half "no." The Bible clearly shows us that God's children should not be divided, but the denominations are obviously divisions. Once we have a denomination, we can see a division. As long as a division exists, do not talk about "spiritual" unity! This behavior lacks thoroughness, as we have already mentioned. We cannot advocate unity on the one hand, yet advocate denominations on the other hand. We cannot keep the divisions on the one hand and talk about unity on the other hand. Just as in the illustrations concerning the cups, the lower half of the picture—the many cups— is wrong, while the upper half of the picture—hands stretched out in fellowship—is right. I think it is clear enough that the Bible says denominations are wrong. Galatians 5:19-21 even lists denominations (sects) as a work of the flesh: "And the works of the flesh are manifest, which are such things as...factions, divisions, sects...."

How does God want us to manifest the unity of the Body? The unity of the Body is not the unity of the whole earth, like the uniting of many churches into one united church; neither is it staying in the denominations and talking about a "spiritual" unity. What is the unity of the Body as spoken of in the Bible? I would like to spend some time to study this matter with you.

The Church Spoken of in Ephesians and Colossians Being Universal Both in Space and in Time

Two Epistles in the Bible especially speak about the church: Ephesians and Colossians. Everyone who studies the Bible knows that the church spoken of in Ephesians and Colossians is the "one church," which is the unique church of

God. This church not only refers to the church on the earth, because even though the church on the earth is broad enough to include everyone according to space, it can only include a section of the church according to time. Suppose five hundred million people are saved on the earth today. The church in the books of Ephesians and Colossians includes more than these five hundred million people. These five hundred million are only the believers in 1951. Before this, in 1950, there were believers who had died. Even in 1951, some believers died before the counting took place. There were also believers who died before 1950, say in 1051. The brothers and sisters in the apostle Paul's time no longer live on this earth today. In other words, the church of Christ in Ephesians and Colossians includes all the saved ones throughout the whole world, in every nation and at all times, both past and present. It covers time as well as space. This is called the Body of Christ. Today, even if all the Christians throughout the whole world are united together, they would still not be the Body of Christ. Although we are living, many have already died; although we are living, many more will be born. Many brothers and sisters will be saved tomorrow. They are in the Body of Christ; we cannot say that they should not be counted. Therefore, the church in any particular period of time on the earth is not the Body of Christ. Even if all the children of God who are on this earth were gathered together, they would not be sufficient to become the Body of Christ. Spacewise it would be sufficient, but timewise it would be wrong to say that it is the Body, because many generations have passed away. All the believers of past generations, all the believers of the present, and all the believers of the future are the Body of Christ.

Ephesians and Colossians speak of the church in this context. This unity is the right spiritual unity. It is impossible to maintain a church with Paul as an elder and Peter as a pastor, because they have passed away. Hence, this unity is spiritual, and this all-encompassing unity is correct. As long as a person is a brother in the Lord, we have fellowship with him. Even though some brothers have passed away, we are still one with them. We are one with any brother or sister.

This is the genuine spiritual unity, which is universal both in time and space.

The Unity Spoken of in 1 Corinthians and Philippians Referring to the Unity of the Church in One Locality

Although we acknowledge the fellowship and unity of Ephesians and Colossians before the Lord, we must remember that this kind of fellowship and unity can easily become idealistic. It is quite possible that we can advocate the unity of the Body on the one hand, yet actually be for the second kind of unity, whereby both denominations and unity are advocated at the same time, on the other hand. Before the Lord, we need to see that the unity of Christians in the Bible is not spoken of in just the Epistles to the Ephesians and Colossians but also in two other Epistles: 1 Corinthians and Philippians. The unity of Christians in these last two Epistles also refers to the unity of the Body.

The unity spoken of in 1 Corinthians clearly does not refer to unity that is universal both in space and in time but to unity of the church in Corinth. I think this word is clear enough. There were contentions among the brothers at Corinth, not the whole Body of Christ. It only concerned a few brothers who were in Corinth. So when Paul exhorted them to be one, he was merely exhorting them to be one with the brothers in their locality. It was as if he was saying, "All the brothers living in Corinth are the church in Corinth; you must express the oneness of the Body in the locality of Corinth. You must not be divided in Corinth."

"You" Referring to the Believers in Corinth

First Corinthians 1:10 says: "Now I beseech you, brothers, through the name of our Lord Jesus Christ, that you all speak the same things..." To whom does *you* refer? It refers to the Christians at Corinth, the brothers at Corinth. "...and that there be no divisions among you..." Again, *you* refers to the Christians at Corinth. "...but that you be attuned in the same mind and in the same opinion." This also refers to the Christians in Corinth. Here we see one thing: If the unity of the Body spoken of in the Bible is not expressed in a locality, it is not practical. It is easy to say, "We love all the children of God, except the one next door! The children of God are one, including Paul and all those who are not yet born, except a few brothers here in Shanghai!" This is impractical as well as self-deceptive. We cannot talk about the unity of the Body and say that we are one with everyone except with the few brothers who live together with us in the same place! According to Paul, *the minimum requirement for speaking of unity is in the context of the local church.* If the Christians in Corinth want to talk about the unity of the Body, they should not talk about it in Rome or talk about it in Jerusalem, but talk about it in Corinth. If we do not talk about it in Corinth, it is useless. We are deceiving ourselves. Suppose I live in Shanghai, but I do not get along with the brothers in Shanghai. However, I get along quite well with the brothers in Nanking. This is useless, and I am deceiving myself. The unity of the Body required by the Scriptures has a minimum boundary requirement, which is the locality. The brothers in Corinth must be one with the brothers in Corinth. If they are not one in Corinth, all their words just deceive others.

"Now I mean this, that each of you says, I am of Paul, and I of Apollos, and I of Cephas, and I of Christ" (v. 12). Note the phrase *each of you.* Who is this? Of course, it is the Corinthians. It would not be right for Paul to speak these words about the brothers in Jerusalem, because the Jerusalem brothers would say that they had not said anything. Neither would it be right if Paul had applied these words to the brothers in Antioch, because they had not said them. Only the brothers in Corinth said them. Here the Lord gives us the light for the most basic form of unity; that is, the believers in Corinth must be one *at least in Corinth.* If unity in Corinth cannot be realized, they should not talk about unity with others. They must be one at least in one place. Perhaps a brother at Corinth can recite the whole book of Ephesians, saying that we must love one another. Of course, we all will love one another in the "heaven" in the future, but the problem is whether or not we love one another today. We all will have fellowship in the "heaven" in the future, but the problem is whether or not we have fellowship today. What we have today is practical. Today in His Word, God's *minimum* requirement for the unity of His children is the locality. If the minimum requirement cannot be met, everything else is false. The brothers who were divided at Corinth said, "You are of Paul, I am of Cephas, he is of Apollos," and someone stood up to say, "I am of Christ." While they were contending among themselves, Paul told them they must be one.

Let us see how Paul rebuked them: "And I, brothers, was not able to speak to you as to spiritual men, but as to fleshy, as to infants in Christ. I gave you milk to drink, not solid food, for you were not yet able to receive it [at the time when you were first saved]. But neither yet now [after being saved for a long time] are you able, for you are still fleshly. For if there is jealousy and strife among you, are you not fleshly and do you not walk according to the manner of man?" (3:1-3). This refers to chapter one. The Corinthians were involved in envy, strife, and divisions; they were fleshly, having the same view of these things as they did when they were first saved. They did not improve at all. When they were first saved, they took milk, but they were still taking milk. If they continued in envy, strife, and divisions, they would be fleshly their whole lives. They would still be drinking milk in their sixties, seventies, and eighties.

The expression of spirituality is in the unity of the church, and the manifestation of the flesh is in the divisions of the church. We cannot call ourselves spiritual and still remain in the divisions. If we are, we are self-deceived. How clear is this word: "For you are still fleshly. For if there is jealousy and strife among you, are you not fleshly and do you not walk according to the manner of man?"

Paul also repeated the words of chapter one in the following verse: "For when someone says, I am of Paul, and another, I of Apollos, are you not men of flesh?" (3:4). He was showing them that divisions are fleshly before God, no matter how good they are before man. The mark of spirituality is oneness; the mark of fleshliness is divisions, envy, and strife.

We must notice that Paul did not pay attention to any

problem arising between the brothers at Corinth and the brothers at Ephesus, or between the brothers at Corinth and the brothers at Colossae. He did not point out any problems between the brothers at Corinth and the brothers at Laodicea, or between the brothers at Corinth and the brothers at Philippi. Paul only paid attention to the divisions between the brothers at Corinth. They said, "I am of Paul, I am of Apollos, I am of Cephas, and I am of Christ," but in effect Paul said, "Brothers! You are brothers at Corinth; you must not have envy, strife, and divisions at Corinth." A boundary does exist. There should not be envy, strife, and divisions in the church at Corinth. To whom does *you* refer? It refers to the church at Corinth. Unity in the Scriptures involves the unity of the Holy Spirit and of the Body. However, the unity of the Holy Spirit and of the Body has a minimum boundary requirement; that is, this unity must be expressed within a local church.

The "Body" Referring to the Children of God in a Certain Time and at a Certain Place

We have just seen the negative view of division; now let us see the positive view of unity as is demanded in the Bible. "We who are many are one Body; for we all partake of the one bread" (1 Cor. 10:17). Here Paul said, "We who are many.... " This includes the children of God at Corinth. This "one bread" is the bread on the table at Corinth. During the breaking of bread at Corinth, a loaf was displayed before the children of God, indicating that though they were many, they were still one bread. In other words, the Body of Christ that the brothers at Corinth should express must at least be expressed *at Corinth*. Here we must recall the situation at that time. Let us take our mind back to the time at Corinth. When the brothers and sisters gathered together, a loaf was displayed before them, with all the saints gathered around it. Perhaps fifty were breaking bread together; Paul was saying that the fifty, being many, are one bread.

In other words, the Body of Christ has a universal expression: the church; this church is the Body of Christ. But the brothers in each locality also express the Body of Christ. It does not mean that the brothers at Corinth are the Body of Christ, while the brothers at Ephesus are not the Body of Christ. It means that the children of God at Corinth are the Body of Christ; so, both according to the spiritual principle and the spiritual fact, they should express themselves as the Body of Christ. The Body of Christ is the universal church, the church which is in all places and throughout all generations both in space and in time. However, the brothers in a locality must at least stand in the same position, applying the same principle to express the same fact. In other words, the minimum boundary of unity is the boundary of locality. In the locality of Corinth, the unity of the Body, the unity of life, must be expressed. This is very wonderful. The Body spoken of in Ephesians refers to all the children of God, but the Body spoken of in Corinthians refers to the children of God in a certain time and at a certain place. The children of God there and then are also the Body of Christ.

As we continue reading 1 Corinthians 12, we see the matter of the Body again. The one Body with the one Holy Spirit is discussed: "For even as the body is one and has many members, yet all the members of the body, being many, are one body, so also is the Christ" (v. 12). "If the foot should say, Because I am not a hand, I am not of the body, it is not that because of this it is not of the body. And if the ear should say, Because I am not an eye, I am not of the body, it is not that because of this it is not of the body....And the eye cannot say to the hand, I have no need of you; nor again the head to the feet, I have no need of you" (vv. 15-16, 21). First Corinthians 12 speaks of the Body of Christ in much detail. The Body of Christ spoken of in 1 Corinthians is different from that which is spoken of in Ephesians. As I have said, the Body of Christ in Ephesians refers to the universal church. This is not a problem to most Bible students. But the Body of Christ in 1 Corinthians 12 refers to the church at Corinth. This is because it is different from that which is spoken of in Ephesians. The Head in Ephesians refers to whom? Ephesians 5:23 says, "Christ is Head of the church." First Corinthians 12 also speaks of the head, but to whom does this refer? First Corinthians 12:21 says, "And the eye cannot say to the hand.... " Here the eye is a member, and the hand is also a member. Verse 21 continues, "...nor again the head to the feet, I have no need of you." The head spoken of in 1 Corinthians 12, therefore, is a member.

This statement cannot be used and applied as an illustration in Ephesians—that would be terrible. A parallel cannot be drawn here. If it were, the Head would be in a very low position. The head in 1 Corinthians 12 is but a member, the position of which is different from that of the Head in Ephesians. The Head in Ephesians is absolutely Christ, while the head in 1 Corinthians 12 is one among the brothers who acts as a head. He is but one of the members, not the unique Head. He is low, not high. Thus, for the expression of the unity of the Body, the Bible shows us that locality is the minimum boundary. I hope the brothers and sisters will see that the minimum requirement of unity in the Bible is the unity of locality. God's children must have spiritual unity in each locality. This is the basic demand of the Bible.

What then is the purpose of God? It is "that there would be no division in the body" (v. 25). Paul said this because of the divisions spoken of in chapters one and three. Paul showed them that having divisions in the locality of Corinth was the same as having divisions in the Body of Christ. Unity must have locality as its boundary. If I live at Corinth, at a minimum I must be one with the children of God in the locality of Corinth; at a minimum I must live out a life that is in oneness at Corinth. I cannot have divisions.

We Must Love the Brothers at Corinth

In chapter thirteen Paul speaks about love. Paul speaks so seriously about love in chapter thirteen because only love is contrary to divisions. Love unites; love does not divide. In Corinth there were envy and strife; so Paul said that love does not envy, does not seek its own things or take account of evil, and does not divide or separate. Paul exhorted the believers in Corinth to at least love one another in the locality of Corinth.

Today a certain kind of condition prevails in the church:

People preach the doctrine of loving one another, but they forget about locality. They feel that the locality is not important. Brothers, it is easy to be idealistic when we preach about loving one another but to forget the matter of locality. It is easy to say, "All the brothers and sisters are lovable except the few in Shanghai!" What should we do? The brothers in Shanghai feel this way; the brothers in Nanking also feel that the brothers are good except for the ones in Nanking. Let me tell you that God says to the brothers in Shanghai: Love the brothers in Shanghai first and the brothers in Nanking later. God also says to the brothers in Nanking: Love the brothers in Nanking first and the brothers in Shanghai later. The brothers in Corinth needed to love the brothers in Corinth first and then they could ascend into heaven to see the Body of Christ. First they needed to descend to see the Body of Christ in 1 Corinthians before they could ascend to see it in Ephesians. They needed to descend to see the Body of Christ in 1 Corinthians because it is much more practical.

If we cannot love the brothers whom we see, how can we love the brothers whom we cannot see? The apostle John said, "He who does not love his brother, whom he has seen, cannot love God, whom he has not seen" (1 John 4:20). Today we need to add one more word: "If we cannot love the brothers whom we see, we cannot love the brothers whom we cannot see." Many do not love the brothers whom they see; they only love the unseen ones. This is what is called "spiritual" fellowship because everything that cannot be seen is "spiritual." If we stand in this position, great difficulties will befall the church. The fellowship among the children of God, the love for one another among the children of God, the care for one another among the children of God, and the oneness among the children of God must start from the locality. *Locality is the minimum requirement.*

The Demand to Be Like-minded in Philippians

In the book of Philippians Paul also exhorted the brothers to be one: "For your fellowship [oneness] unto the furtherance of the gospel from the first day until now" (1:5). Later, Paul spoke of another aspect in verses 15 and 17: "Some preach Christ even because of envy and strife....others announce Christ out of selfish ambition." This was not a universal condition of the church but a local matter in Philippi. Some brothers preached Christ in oneness, while some preached Christ out of envy, saying, "If you can preach, I can too. If you can do it, why cannot I?" So they also preached.

In Philippians 2:2 Paul exhorted, "Think the same thing, having the same love, joined in soul, thinking the one thing." I would like to point out the phrase *that you think the same thing*. This does not refer to the universal church. Although the universal church can learn from this instance, this word especially refers to the Philippians, since Paul wrote the letter to the Philippians. The Christians, the brothers, in Philippi needed to think the same thing. It is useless for them to think the same thing as the brothers in the church in Shanghai or the brothers in the church in Lanchow. They have to think the same thing as the brothers in Philippi. This is the commandment of the Bible. Thinking the same thing must have locality as its minimum requirement. If this is lacking, all doctrines are idealistic and imaginary. It is amazing that many brothers are very spiritual in the heavens, but fleshly on earth. Their idea is very spiritual but their practice is fleshly.

Following this, Paul said that if they thought the same thing, had the same love, were joined in soul, and thought the one thing, his joy would be made full.

"Doing nothing by way of selfish ambition" (v. 3a). This word was spoken to the Philippians. The Philippians should not have done anything by way of selfish ambition. Paul brought out the reason for doing things by selfish ambition: Some covet vainglory. These seekers of vainglory are easily separated from the brothers. Those who desire to have glory before man get into trouble with others. Some are proud and esteem themselves highly; they are unable to be one with others. "But in lowliness of mind considering one another more excellent than yourselves" (v. 3b). This will enable us to be one with others. Some care only for their own things and are very selfish; so it is also easy for them to cause trouble.

Paul continued, "Not regarding each his own virtues, but each the virtues of others also" (v. 4). This is the reason that many people cannot think the same thing, cannot have the same love, cannot be joined in soul, cannot be one with others. Some care only for themselves, some are proud, some seek glory and desire others to applaud them. These kinds of people can never be one with others. We must learn to be humble, not seeking glory from man, and we must learn to take care of others. Then we can be one with other children of God. This is the scriptural principle, and we need to follow it accordingly.

Paul praised the Philippians for their fellowship (oneness) in preaching the gospel, but in fact, they had contentions. This made the exhortation in chapter two necessary. There were contentions in Philippi not only among the brothers but also among the sisters. In chapter four Paul especially mentioned two sisters: "I exhort Euodias, and I exhort Syntyche, to think the same thing in the Lord" (v. 2). These two names are feminine. We do not know how much of a story lies behind this word; Paul did not reveal this to us. He only said, "I exhort Euodias, and I exhort Syntyche, to think the same thing in the Lord." This correction shows us on the one hand that there was strife in Philippi, and on the other hand that this strife was limited to this locality because of the names he mentioned. By now I think we should see at least one thing: The unity of the Body or the unity of the Holy Spirit in the Bible refers to the unity in locality. Unity apart from locality is entirely vain. We cannot say that we are able to be one everywhere except in our own locality.

The Church in the Bible Being Local

Now we shall go on to see the reason we stress the expression of unity in locality. This is because the church in the Bible is local. We have spoken about this for many years and have mentioned it even now a number of times. The church in the Bible is local. A single exception cannot be seen in the whole New Testament. All the churches are local: the church in Jerusalem, the church in Antioch, the church in Corinth, the church in Philippi, the church in Colossae, etc. All the examples in the Bible are local. For example, in the book of Revelation, the churches in Ephesus, Smyrna, Pergamos, Thyatira, Sardis, Philadelphia, and Laodicea are all local. *God ordained one church in each locality.* The localities and the churches are equal to each other. The countries on the earth are divided into cities; the church of God on the earth today is also divided into cities. In the world there is the locality of Shanghai; hence, there is a church in Shanghai before God. In the world there is a locality of Nanking; hence, there is the church in Nanking before God. In the world there are the localities of Sian and Lanchow; hence, there is the church in Sian and the church in Lanchow before God. As long as there is a place big enough to be a locality, there should be a church in that locality. If our place is not big enough to be a locality, we cannot be a church. Lanchow is big enough in the eyes of God to be a locality; therefore, there can be a church in Lanchow. Before God this matter is very clear.

The Bible determines a locality according to the limit of a city or a village. In 1 Corinthians for example, which we have just read, there is a very good word: "Because of this I have sent Timothy to you, who is my beloved and faithful child in the Lord, who will remind you of my ways which are in Christ, even as I teach everywhere in every church" (4:17). "Everywhere" is the locality; "every church" is the spiritual content. In every locality there is a church. "Everywhere" is divided in the Bible according to a city or a village. The Lord Jesus preached the gospel in every city and in every village (Matt. 9:35); therefore, the unit of locality is the city or village. Paul said to Titus, "Appoint elders in every city, as I directed you" (Titus 1:5). During that time Paul preached the gospel in the cities; he had not gone into the villages. Hence, he did not mention villages. All the churches in the Bible are local. This is the problem today: The unity of the children of God must have locality as its unit. In other words, the minimum unit for the unity of the children of God must be the unit of locality. All the children of God in the same locality must be one. This is the minimum requirement.

There Should Be Spiritual Fellowship between the Churches

Now I wish to discuss a problem which God's children face in connection with this matter. I have already spoken of the second kind of unity, part of which is right and part of which is wrong. What does this mean? Should there be the "spiritual fellowship" they talk about? Part of it should exist, and part of it should not. The way to fulfill the part that should exist is that there should be spiritual fellowship between one local church and another local church. The Bible shows us that the church is local, so there must be the unity of the church in a locality. Therefore, I have said that if there is no unity in a locality, all other words are vain and self-deceptive. Fellowship among the churches does not mean that a locality neglects its own affairs and takes care of the affairs of another locality. It does not mean that the brothers in Tiensui take care of the affairs of Pingliang but not the affairs in Tiensui. Rather, it means that Tiensui and Pingliang should have fellowship in spiritual matters.

The unity of the church, the unity of the Body, has locality as its unit. But we also must have spiritual unity with brothers in other localities. This spiritual unity is not a unity between one denomination and another denomination, but a unity between one church and another church. This spiritual unity is not a unity between divisions, but the unity between members of the Body. Here are two local churches. Between these two local churches, we should seek the unity of the Holy Spirit, the unity of the Body, the unity in the Lord's way, and unity in every aspect in order to express the spiritual unity between the churches. If we apply this spiritual unity to the denominations instead of to the churches, this is wrong. It is wrong to place spiritual unity in the context of the sects instead of in the context of the localities. The subject is right, but the application is wrong.

The Unity of Congregationalism

Now let us see the importance of the boundary of locality. Perhaps we first should look at history. We have seen that in the beginning the churches in the Bible were local. Later, these churches were united to form provincial or district churches. Still later, they were united into an international church under the pope. When the churches were harmonious with God's purpose in the beginning, they were local. Gradually, however, they degraded until there was only one church in the whole world, the Roman Catholic Church. During the Reformation, the Roman Catholic Church was broken up. In this breaking apart, the original local churches were not restored. Subsequent to this breaking apart, the international church became national churches with state churches in different nations. There was some improvement, some advancement, at this stage, with the churches being somewhat closer to the likeness of those in the beginning. The state churches later became independent churches. Within a nation, there were scores, hundreds, and even thousands of small churches. These independent churches took another step closer to the situation in the beginning.

We must realize how difficult it was for these independent churches to be established. For example, the church in many nations insisted that sermons could only be preached in holy places. These holy places were the dedicated sanctuaries. John Wesley rose up and said that preaching could be done anywhere. He was greatly persecuted! The state church declared that messages preached in undedicated places were defiled. In addition to the place being dedicated, the person preaching the message had to be ordained; no ordinary person was allowed to preach. This is the reason Darby said that Paul, Peter, and John could not have preached according to this view, because they were not ordained. For the state churches, preaching was serious, location was serious, and setting up new churches was even more serious. Even Luther, during the Reformation, dared not establish a church. It was the political power that forced him to do so. Nevertheless, after Wesley was raised up, the climate gradually changed as independent churches were established. The international church had evolved into national churches, and the national churches had evolved into independent churches.

Among these independent churches, a doctrine that became quite prevalent was the so-called congregationalism, which means that every independent congregation is a church. Who believed in congregationalism? It was the Congregationalists and the Baptists. What is meant by congregationalism? Many children of God among them in their reading of the Bible saw that the churches were all independent of one another. The church in Jerusalem had its own administration, the church in Antioch took care of its own affairs, and the church in Corinth, as well as the church in Ephesus, also had its own administration. Although the church was universal, they thought that each congregation was the unit of church administration. Hence, it was called "congregationalism." They set up congregational churches with each congregation serving as a church. There was no archbishop above them. Compared with the other independent churches, this was an improvement. Now we see progress in these various stages; the international church improved to become national churches, national churches improved to become independent churches, and some independent churches improved to become congregational churches.

The Mistake of Congregationalism

Congregationalism is actually very close to the Bible, but it goes a little beyond the Bible. The Congregationalist brothers studied the Bible but failed to discover the thought of *locality*. Jerusalem is a city, not a congregation; Antioch is a city, not a congregation; Ephesus is a port city, not a congregation; Colossae is a city on a hill, not a congregation. They thought that Jerusalem, Antioch, Ephesus, and Colossae were congregations, and they concluded that congregations were independent of each other. Church history tells us that not long after its beginning, the church deteriorated until the time of Luther. Afterward there was a recovery, an improvement, until the stage of the independent churches. From the time of the independent churches, the church went to another extreme of taking a congregation as the unit. This included Congregationalists and Baptists and later even the Open

Brethren who also went to the extreme of considering a congregation as the unit.

Now I wish to discuss the reason that congregationalism is wrong. It is the closest to the Bible; yet it is still wrong. The Lord desires that we love one another, receive one another, and avoid envy, strife, and divisions in the same local church. The unity of congregationalism takes the congregation as its unit. This poses a problem in that it is difficult to pin down such a thing as a congregation. There may be one congregation at 145 Nanyang Road and another at 143 Nanyang Road. If I love the brothers at 145 Nanyang Road, I will meet with them. When I disagree with them, I will set up another congregation at 143 Nanyang Road. If we have seen that unity is a matter of locality, we could only go and set up a church in another city, not another one in Shanghai. This is not easy, but still we must love one another. Oh, how great is the Lord's wisdom in putting us in localities and giving us the locality as the boundary! Only here can we really find the cross to bear and the lessons to learn.

What is the meaning of a congregational church? It means that there can be several congregations within each locality, each having a unity within itself and each independent of the others. This is a very serious matter. The unity of congregationalism is a mistake. The mistake of the international church goes to one extreme, causing many localities to have one church, but the mistake of the congregational churches goes to the opposite extreme, causing one locality to have many churches. The Roman Catholic Church is at one end, with many localities having one church, and the congregational churches are at the other end, with one locality having many churches. This is like a pendulum that swings to one side with many localities having one church and then swings to the other side with one locality having five to ten churches. In the last century the Brethren were raised up, but some of them fell into congregationalism. They were mainly separated into the Closed Brethren and the Open Brethren. The Closed Brethren are still on the side of the united church; the Open Brethren have gone to the other side and become congregations, "chapel" assemblies. They may have one assembly on one street and another assembly on another street, each having nothing to do with the other. This means they have many churches in one locality.

One Locality with One Church

Therefore, we must see clearly before God that in the Bible there is one locality with one church, or in short, one locality, one church. This is the principle in the Bible. If we study the matter of the church, we must be able to understand this principle of one locality, one church. Every mistake comes from violating this principle. One locality, one church is the pendulum. When it swings to one side, it is wrong because it causes three or four localities to have one church or the whole world to have one church. When it swings to the opposite side, it is also wrong because it causes one locality to have several or many churches. There is something abnormal in connection with the locality, or there is something abnormal in connection with the church. In the Bible there is one locality, one church. At the time of the apostles, the population of the city of Jerusalem was about one million. It was one of the most highly populated cities. Many localities in China today are still not as highly populated. At that time three thousand people were saved and then five thousand (Acts 2:41; 4:4). The number of the saved eventually reached several tens of thousands of people (21:20). That was really unusual. Since there was no place large enough for them to meet together, they met from house to house. However, the Bible does not speak of "the churches in Jerusalem." I doubt whether they could easily find a meeting place large enough for three to five thousand to gather together. It may be that all these people did not meet together even once. It could be that they met in the wilderness; we do not know. Although the city was very large and there were many believers, they were still *one* church. Hence, the Bible shows us *one locality, one church.*

We have seen clearly that the Roman Catholic Church has swung to one side with the principle of having one church with many localities. Another group of people are on the other side with the principle of one locality having many churches. In the same locality, you are one church and others are another. This is congregationalism. It is enough to love those in the same congregation and not care for the other congregation. The Open Brethren have gone in the direction of the congregational church; the Closed Brethren have gone in the direction of the Roman Catholic Church.

Thus, we face a huge problem in China. We must maintain a testimony against the work of the Roman Catholic Church on one hand and the work of congregational churches on the other hand. If we are just a little careless, congregationalism will appear. If we are clear that there is one locality, one church, then we will be clear about Roman Catholicism and congregationalism. For instance, Sian is a locality; therefore, there should be one church there. Regardless of whether the church in Sian is good or bad, it is the one church there. If I am right with the brothers in Sian, I am in the church in Sian; if I am not right with the brothers in Sian, I am still in the church in Sian.

Now let us see the consequences of congregationalism. If I am a believer of congregationalism and I am right with the brothers, then I will break bread with them; if I am not, we will break bread separately because you love your group and I love my group. This kind of breaking of bread costs nothing; it is unnecessary to hire a pastor. We can just set up a table as we like and break bread. We can form another church, love one another, wash one another's feet from morning to evening, have a love feast at every meal, and have very good fellowship. But the Bible says one locality, one church. The Bible says that "we [the saints in the same locality] who are many are...one bread" (1 Cor. 10:17). But what are you? You, being few, are two loaves. You say, "We are one loaf and you also are a loaf"—this is congregationalism. It is a dreadful situation for the church once congregationalism appears. Roman Catholicism over a period of eleven hundred years had but one church. If congregationalism exists for a period of eleven hundred years, there may be hundreds and thousands of churches. Those who like contentions always seek causes of contention. Suppose I am contentious and have found a brother to contend with. The contention will end in a division. Then I will suffer because I will have no one to contend with;

so I will look for someone else. This is appalling; the church
will not only be divided into many pieces but will also advocate divisions. If the principle is wrong, difficulties will
follow: once a disagreement occurs, you will set up a table and
another will set up another table.

The Lord has shown us that *one locality should have only
one church, and one locality should have only one administration.* So we must be limited by locality. If any brother is not
one with me, I must wash his feet and beg him until he
becomes one with me. Here are lessons for me to learn: My
temper has to be dealt with; I need to find the reason a
brother cannot be one with me and do my best to deal with it;
otherwise, there will be no way for us to go on. If we act
according to congregationalism, it is very convenient. Once
anything disagreeable occurs, I will set up another church.
Then in Shanghai there may not only be twenty-four home
meetings, but twenty-four churches. Consequently, one locality with many churches will appear. This is a very serious
matter. There is a boundary to our unity. The unity of the
Roman Catholic Church is against the Scriptures, and "spiritual" unity has come short of the Lord's goal. The unity in the
Scriptures is according to one locality with one church. This
makes it impossible not to be one in each locality.

Suppose there are a few brothers with whom the church
really seeks oneness. We should find out what their attitude
is. Within these few days I have heard someone say, "We can
talk and fellowship, even though you can still have your
church, I have my church, and he has his church. We all are
one; we all stand in our own position to be one with each
other. We all have our own elders and deacons, yet we respect
one another." I must tell these brothers emphatically that
there is only one church in one locality. These ones' thought of
rallying brothers together from a few denominations in a
locality will only please a few churches. You may deal with
the past and deal with it quite well with your cleverness,
but what will you do with the future? We all will eventually
pass away. What would you have the younger brothers do
in the future? If our brothers practice congregationalism in
every place, tolerating this kind of unity, to say nothing of

sacrificing our obedience, what shall we do in the future? We may get by with five congregations today, but there will be some difficulty in the future, and with it a sixth congregation will appear. With more difficulties, a seventh and eighth will appear. What will we do then? We all must see this basic principle. The Lord's commandment is very clear: On the one hand, He will not allow us to have a united church so that we will not become a power on the earth and among men. On the other hand, He will not allow a church to become several churches in one locality; otherwise, future contentions will be endless.

I would like you to see that congregationalism is the result of brothers seeing the truth in the Bible only in part. There is no congregationalism in the Bible. Jerusalem, Antioch, Ephesus, Thyatira, and Laodicea are all localities. Throughout many years of church history, the Lord's light has become clearer and clearer: from the international church to the national church, from the national church to the independent church, and from the independent church, somewhat beyond the normal standard, to congregationalism. Within these last twenty to thirty years, the Lord has led us to see the local church. It is clear enough. The church today is taking the apostles' way. The church is local. We should not be proud to say that this is preached by us. This is the grace of God. God allowed His children to grope for more than a thousand years. Thank God! We have inherited what they gained and have found the way. Thank God! Although Congregationalism is wrong, it is an improvement. They saw that the "one church" of Roman Catholicism is wrong, but their improvement is beyond the standard.

Even such good brothers as the Brethren had contentions because one group of the Brethren took the way of the united church and another group took the way of the congregations. The China Inland Mission also practices congregationalism. Today the most prevailing practice is congregationalism. The little booklet written by Goodman entitled *An Urgent Cry* is also something of congregationalism. What is congregationalism? It is when there is an assembly on a certain street and also one nearby, each of which does not care for the other, whether the other is doing well or doing poorly. The only unity they seek is a unity within their own assembly. As long as they all can be one with each other, they meet together as one assembly; otherwise, they divide. The loving of one another as advocated by congregationalism is this kind of love; it is not limited by locality and does not attempt to learn its lessons within a locality. This is the reason I have said again and again that the lessons to be learned within a locality are an exceedingly severe matter. We live in this city, and it is not easy for us to move away. The Lord has placed us in a certain locality to thoroughly grind us. We cannot act as we like. Hence, we have lessons to learn and the cross to bear. Otherwise, there is no cross for us to bear; in just a few days we will throw away the cross.

We must see that Paul was against congregationalism in 1 Corinthians. Corinth is a city, and there was only one church in Corinth. "The church of God which is in Corinth" (1:2) is singular according to the Greek text. But how did the Corinthian brothers behave? They said, "I am of Paul, and I of Apollos, and I of Cephas, and I of Christ" (v. 12). In other words, the one church was divided into four congregations. Those of Paul loved and came together with those of Paul. Those of Apollos found it easy to love and come together with those of Apollos. Those of Cephas came together with others of Cephas. And those of Christ came together with others of Christ and loved one another. But Paul said they were all fleshly, they were all men of flesh (1 Cor. 3:3-4). They were not of Paul, not of Apollos, not of Cephas, and not of Christ, but of the flesh. Paul would not allow them to belong to him, Apollos would not allow them to belong to him, Cephas would not allow them to belong to him, and neither would Christ allow them to belong to Him. They belonged to the flesh. There can be only one church in a city. The desire to be divided into parties or sects within the church is all of the flesh. According to the Bible, we should maintain nothing less than the unity of a church in one locality. Any unity smaller than this is inadmissible.

If we see this accurately before the Lord, we could say a very precise word to the brothers in the denominations. For example, in Pingliang and in Tiensui there can be only one church in each locality. Show them the Bible, regardless of which verse you use about the church, and ask them whether or not the church is local. In the past there was Corinth; today there is Pingliang. This transition is quite reasonable. In the past there was Ephesus; today there is Tiensui. This is also very reasonable. In the past there was one church in a locality; it should not be changed to several churches today. I know that many brothers are turning back to congregationalism today. Not long ago brothers in Shanghai advocated home churches. Quite simply, this is still congregationalism. Hence, we all must be clear to maintain one locality, one church. The pendulum should not swing to one side or to the other. According to the definition of a home church, each home meeting is a church. Thus, we have "churches" in Shanghai. If this could be so, then not only would there have been seven churches in Asia, but there could have been four churches in Corinth. There could be seven churches in Asia because Asia was a province; but there could not be four churches in Corinth because Corinth was a city. The Corinthians said, "I am of Paul, and I of Apollos, and I of Cephas, and I of Christ"; therefore, Paul said they were fleshly. The church is only one; it is impossible to have four churches in one locality. Once this problem is solved, all other problems are solved.

We Must Fear More to Found a Church than to Do Anything

Finally, we must pay attention to another problem. We have seen that the unity of the Body is expressed in the locality. If we do not pay attention to the unity in the locality, then other kinds of unity are vain words because they are not found in the Bible. Unity must be expressed in locality; otherwise, it is vain to talk about it. Unity must not wait until we go to heaven to be realized because we will all be one in heaven. Unity is being one with the brothers around us today. Otherwise, the error of congregationalism will follow. Those in the Roman Catholic Church have learned something about the church, but they have applied it incorrectly. Everyone in the Roman Catholic Church has seen that the church is one, but they are mistaken about the boundary. They think that there is only one church on the earth. What about us? In one point we are the same as they because we have seen that the church is one. However, they have one church for the whole earth; we have one church for each locality. Since Roman Catholicism believes that there is only one church in the whole earth, they have learned the lesson of not setting up another kind of church. This is a good point. No matter how great their difficulties are, they still stay together and dare not divide. Since they have seen that the church is one, they feel that they would be sinning against the Lord if they brought forth divisions. Today as we learn the same lesson, I expect to see the same kind of result, namely, that *we will also not dare to set up other churches,* but instead remain with the brothers to learn the same lesson.

I do not know how to speak to the brothers today. I feel we should learn our lesson so well before the Lord that we can do anything *except set up another church.* When we move to a locality, we may have the liberty to found a school, a hospital, a seminary, a corporation, or a factory. We may have the freedom to do anything. Even if it is not of the Lord, this is not the greatest sin. I am not saying that we should be disobedient to the Lord's will, but I am saying that such a mistake is not the greatest one. Certainly, however, *we should never go out to set up another church.* Setting up churches according to our own wishes is the greatest sin. We must fear founding a church more than anything else.

Brothers, do we see the seriousness of this matter? Nothing is worse than setting up a church at will. We can found anything, but we must never establish a church in this manner because this involves the problem of the Body of Christ. We must be clear about this matter before God.

Wherever we go, we first must find *whether or not a church exists* in that locality. It is not a matter of whether or not the church there is strong. That is another matter. It does not matter whether or not the church there is spiritual. That is a secondary matter. If there is a denomination at this end or a Roman Catholic Church at the other end, if there are many churches in one locality or one church in many localities, then there is not a church in that locality, and we can set up a church there. Because the church is local, it is neither congregationalism nor unionism. If there is a local church in a locality, we must not set up another. We must fear setting up another table for the breaking of bread. This is a terrible thing.

My heart is aching today because of those who have read some of our books and have seen a little about the truth of the church and then say, "Let us meet together." Brothers, it is not so simple! We cannot set up a church loosely at our pleasure. First, we need to see whether or not a church exists in our locality. If a local church already exists, then we must communicate with them even if we are unwilling. If there is a denomination or a sect, we cannot join it because we cannot stand in the denominations. But if there is a local church, we cannot set up another one under the pretense of helping it, even though we see some faults in it. We can only help it through teaching, not through setting up another church. My heart grieves because many people are not afraid of setting up another church. They presume that this is a very simple matter and that they can immediately set up a church after discussing it with three or four others. Brothers who are somewhat gifted, who have some scriptural knowledge, and who are capable in preaching, think that they can set up a church. I may have some trouble with my brothers, and it would not be difficult for me to go out to preach, to set up the Lord's table, and to build a meeting hall. But I could never do this, because the church is one in each locality.

Therefore, brothers, we must be brought to the place today that we would never commit the sin of dividing the Body of Christ. There is only one Body of Christ. I do not want to be such a carnal person, a person of the flesh, causing divisions. When the brothers all stand in this position, our learning will increase and our spirituality will increase. We will be led to the pathway of the church, and all the brothers and sisters will have the real unity—not a big, outward unity that is obscure within, neither a "spiritual" unity that allows us to remain in divisions.

The booklet *The Urgent Cry* speaks of the unity in Christ that exists for one week every year at the Keswick Convention in England. I wish to ask, however, about the other fifty-one weeks of the year. If we are one in Christ, we should be one throughout all fifty-two weeks of the year. If we should be divided, then we should be divided all fifty-two weeks. But the strange thing is that the unity at Keswick lasts one week out of the year. Then everyone returns to the divisions. Some brothers still regard this as an example of unity. However, if we should be divided, we should be divided all the time. If we should keep the unity, we should keep it all the time. Either we unite or we divide. If we can only be united for a week, while being divided for the rest of the year, we would rather stay at Keswick every day and never leave. We must see a thorough and absolute unity, not a so-called "spiritual" unity. The term is good, but it is applied in a wrong sense. The unity we see is the unity of the Body of Christ *expressed in the locality*. This expression *in the locality*, however, stumbles many people. This is a great test. Of course, if God were to remove the word *locality*, then everything would be easy. We could hold a few meetings for everyone to come together and converse and then return to the divisions.

I wish the brothers in China today would see that the church is local. Later, by God's mercy, we may have several hundred or several thousand local churches raised up. The churches may also spread to foreign countries, to turn back to the Western world from where the gospel came. I hope our brothers in China will not be influenced by congregationalism. There is nothing in congregationalism but one word— division. It divides a locality into many divisions. I hope the brothers and sisters will have a fearful heart in setting up new churches, daring to do anything but set up a church. We must seriously see that the Body of Christ is expressed in the locality. Of course, we cannot force others to take this way. If there is a denomination in a locality, that is another matter. If there is a division in a locality, that is also another matter. But if there is already a church in that locality, we must not establish another church. If we do this, I think the church in China will have a better way to go on.

A Problem concerning Unity

A brother asked, "As the word concerning the unity of the church goes out from us at this time, people may very easily misunderstand that we are asking others to unite with us. Why do we not unite with them?"

In order to answer this question, we must let them know the basic problem: Before the Lord we can yield in certain things, but there are other matters in which we can never compromise. What are the things concerning which we cannot compromise? They are the teachings of the Bible because they are the Word of God. Even if we want to compromise, we still cannot. It is not just a matter of saying things one way as opposed to another; we cannot alter the Word of God. In what things can we yield? We can yield in our own position, but toward brothers who are in the denominations, whether in a congregational church or a united church, there are things which we cannot compromise. In these things we should stand firm and should not compromise. However, in things in which we can give in, we should yield because we must seek unity.

There are two points in which we cannot compromise: 1) Denominations are sin; hence, we cannot compromise in this. God said that divisions (sects, denominations) are of the flesh. We cannot say that divisions are spiritual. If we are not faithful to the Lord, we are not His servants and cannot preach His words. Denominationalism is always to be condemned. This is the negative aspect. 2) We must ask them to acknowledge that the church is local. This is the positive aspect with which we can never compromise. There should be only one church in each locality, not several churches. This is the Word of the Lord, and we have no authority to alter it. We cannot change one or the other. Once the problem regarding the Word of the Lord is settled, there is no problem whether you should unite with me or I should unite with you. This will not involve the Word of the Lord; it will only involve our position. If one considers only his position, he is wrong and is not the servant of the Lord.

If others are united with us today, how about divisions

that may occur in the future? Since they have just started to walk this way, it may be quite easy for trouble to arise again. For those who have done something once, it is extremely easy to do it again. For those who have walked in the way of denominations, it is very easy to walk in that way again. It is not that we do not trust our brothers but that they must condemn denominationalism as sin. Then God will deliver them out of it. If they do not condemn the denominationalism as sin, even though they have come out of it, trouble will arise in the future. Furthermore, if we maneuver to attain unity, problems will arise. We must not relax these two points: Denominationalism is sin, and the church is local. We can tell these ones that we have been walking in this way for thirty years and that we hope they also will walk together with us.

On the other hand, it is all right for us to consider ourselves as not having walked in this way and starting all over again. In spite of our history, it is all right for us to join others. The Word of the Lord is the Lord's and we cannot give it up, but we can give up our history. The church is local and denominationalism is sin; we cannot relax on these two points. However, we can have a new start tomorrow in regard to our position. If we reject the denominations and they reject the denominations, then we can unite together to become the local church. How about that? Our history is something we can give up, and we can start all over again. We can say that they are not the church and that we are not the church, but that tomorrow we all will be the church. How about this? We will give up anything that can be given up, but the Lord's Word cannot be given up; we cannot relinquish it. This problem is easily settled; this is not a difficulty.

As to the administration, there also can be only one in each locality. Congregationalism has several administrations in each locality. Acts 14:23 says that Paul and Barnabas appointed elders in every church. If this were the only record in the Bible regarding Paul's action, people could say that it is possible to have several churches in one locality and elders in each one of these churches. However, if we read Titus 1:5, we will see that the situation is different. Paul said, "Appoint elders in every city." When we bring these two texts together, we will see that they are very specific. One text says "in every church"; the other text says "in every city." Therefore, elders are ordained for every church, and the city is the boundary for the elders' administration in the church.

Many brothers and sisters think that having unity with us is only a spiritual matter and that their administration will still be independent. This is not the teaching of the Scriptures. Every locality must have *only one church and only one administration;* it is impossible to have several churches and several administrations in one locality. Since this is a very important matter, we must be clear about it. There can only be one administration in one city, not several administrations. If we are clear about this, there will be little problem. Otherwise, when we have trouble in one meeting, we will go to another meeting. If one meeting does not receive us, we can go to another meeting on another street and be received. If the children of God have seen the unity of the church, the brothers and sisters will be one not only in fellowship but in administration as well.

CHAPTER FIVE

THE SERVICE OF THE CHURCH

(Parts of two talks given by Brother Watchman Nee to the co-workers as trainees on Mount Kuling in the year 1948. The first part was published in April 1949, in chapter forty-nine of *Messages for Building Up New Believers,* and the second part published in March 1950, in the third chapter of *Church Affairs.*)

If the church has the proper ground outwardly and the proper content inwardly, it is still insufficient. She must also have the service, the service of the church.

The service of the church has been neglected through all these generations. Even today we do not have an adequate realization concerning it.

The service of the church is a spiritual coordination, a coordination of the saints in life and in the Holy Spirit. It is the spiritual activity of the saints, who are members one of another in the Holy Spirit, as one Body, each member functioning according to its office. It is not the independent movement of an individual, but the coordinated movement of all the saints. It is not the service of one person individually, but the serving together of all the saints. It is not the service of one pastor plus a preacher and several elders and deacons, but the service in which all the saints participate together.

If a church is normal, the number of people saved should also be the number of people serving. In the New Testament, all the saved ones are priests; therefore, all the saved ones should serve. If in a church only a minority or a part are serving, there is something wrong with that church; it is still weak. Only when all are serving is the church strong.

SERVICE IN THE BODY

First Corinthians 12:14-21 says, "For the body is not one member but many. If the foot should say, Because I am not a hand, I am not of the body, it is not that because of this it is not of the body....If the whole body were an eye, where would the hearing be? If the whole were the hearing, where would the smelling be? But now God has placed the members, each one of them, in the body, even as He willed. And if all were one member, where would the body be? But now the members are many, but the body one. And the eye cannot say to the hand, I have no need of you; nor again the head to the feet, I have no need of you." Verses 28 through 30 go on to say, "And God has placed some in the church: first apostles, second prophets, third teachers; then works of power, then gifts of healing, helps, administrations, various kinds of tongues. Are all apostles? Are all prophets? Are all teachers? Do all have works of power? Do all have gifts of healing? Do all speak in tongues? Do all interpret tongues?"

There are many members in the Body of Christ, and the Holy Spirit dispenses all kinds of gifts and ministries to them according to the need of the Body. The Lord grants the members different kinds of gifts and ministries for the purpose of supplying the need of the whole Body. The Lord knows that He will not make the whole Body the eyes or the whole Body the ears. The Lord gives the members different gifts and ministries to supply the whole Body. As the human body needs all the members, so the church needs the different kinds of gifts and ministries for its spiritual service. Some serve in the ministry of the word. Some serve by performing works of power. Some exercise the gift of healing. Some render helps. Some speak in tongues and some interpret tongues, etc. The church must provide ample opportunity for all the brothers and sisters to serve. All the members, including the uncomely ones, are useful in the ministry of the Spirit. It is impossible to have a useless member in the Body. Every brother and sister is a member in the Body and every member has his or her function and service. As long as you are a Christian, you are a member of the Body of Christ, and as a member in the Body, you must have your own service before God. We must honor such a practice of universal service. Every Christian must have his or her respective function and must serve the Lord according to this function.

Every member in the church should find a place to serve. Everyone should serve and there should not be any monopoly. A member or a few members should not replace all the members in doing everything. Any system that does not provide opportunity for all the members to function is surely not of the Body. In the physical body, the eyes, the mouth, the feet, and the hands may all be very busy. Yet they do not contradict each other. Something is wrong if only the eyes function while the mouth, feet, and hands do not. If the eyes, mouth, feet, and hands all function together and coordinate as one entity, we have the body. If some serve and others do not or if only one or a few serve, we do not have the Body of Christ. We must be very clear about this principle.

Romans 12:4-8 says, "For just as in one body we have many members, and all the members do not have the same function, so we who are many are one body in Christ, and individually members one of another. And having gifts that differ according to the grace given to us, whether prophecy, let us prophesy according to the proportion of faith; or service, let us be faithful in that service; or he who teaches, in that teaching; or he who exhorts, in that exhortation; he who gives, in simplicity; he who leads, in diligence; he who shows mercy, in cheerfulness."

Another matter which requires special attention in the Body is that both the grace and the gift that everyone receives are different. The passage in 1 Corinthians 12 emphasizes the ministry of the word and the miraculous gifts. The passage in Romans 12, in addition to speaking of the ministry of the word, includes ministries of other services in the church as well. Some give, some lead, and some show mercy. All these can be considered works of the Levites. They are services that pertain to practical affairs.

Romans 12 shows us that everyone who is gifted must function according to the gift which God has given him, whether it is in the ministry of the word or in the ministry of service. He who prophesies, let him prophesy. He who serves, let him serve. He who teaches, let him teach. He who exhorts, let him exhort. He who leads, let him lead diligently in the church. In other words, everyone should serve. Everyone should have his or her specific service and should be faithful to this function. Everyone should know what he can do before God and what gift he has received from the Lord. This knowledge should direct him to function in a specific way. No one should go beyond his own function to take over the service of others. No member should take the place of another member, and no member should relinquish his own function. All should serve together, and everyone should fully apply himself to his own work. In this way the Body of Christ will be expressed.

The Body cannot allow one member to neglect his duty. The whole Body is in darkness if the eyes do not see. The whole Body cannot walk if the feet refuse to walk. The eyes should see and the feet should walk. Even though the gift that you have received from God may be small, you should not hide your gift. Even if the gift you have received from God is just one talent (Matt. 25:14-30), you should not keep it or neglect it. Whether one's gift is big or small, whether it is "five talents," "two talents," or "one talent," he should exercise what he has and serve accordingly. If he refuses to give himself to his service and instead buries his "one talent," the church will suffer. If a few members in the Body refuse to function, the Body will suffer great loss.

It is not easy to find five-talented ones in the church. Yet every child of God, no matter how small his gift may be, has at least one talent. If all the one-talented ones will rise up to serve, they will be more effective than the few who have five talents. If all the one-talented ones will rise up to serve, the church will surely flourish. All those with one talent should rise up to serve. Whether or not the church will prosper depends on whether the one-talented ones will rise up to serve. If only a few people are laboring and working, we do not have the church. If all the brothers and sisters are working and laboring, it will be the church serving and the Body functioning. A few members no longer will take over the function of the whole Body. We hope everyone who has "one talent" will dig out his talent from the earth. Everyone who has the "mina" should realize that the handkerchief is for wiping sweat, not for wrapping up his mina (Luke 19:20). We must learn to serve according to our ability. When everyone rises up to serve and no one passes his responsibility to someone else, we have the church.

ALL SHOULD LEARN

With regard to the practical affairs of the church, the brothers and sisters must be very concerned and very clear. Regardless of what kind of affair it is, all must put their hand to it. For example, the cleaning of the meeting place and the care and arrangement of the blankets and sheets that belong to the church are all in the nature of the service of the Levites. The care of those who are needy among us and the receiving and sending off of visiting brothers and sisters are also work in the nature of the Levitical service. There is a great amount of work in the nature of the Levitical service. There is much work in the church service office, which is also Levitical.

When a person serves God, there is the priestly work on the one hand, and there is the Levitical work on the other hand. Both should be accomplished. On the one hand, you participate in the spiritual service, and on the other hand, you should also take care of the practical affairs. Remember that Stephen and some others took care of serving food. That was the service of the deacons, the work of the Levites. When the disciples distributed the loaves and collected twelve baskets of fragments and on another occasion collected seven baskets of fragments, they were doing the work of the deacons. In particular, Judas's responsibility for the purse was the business of the deacons. The Lord Jesus at the well at Sychar sent His disciples away to buy food. Their buying of food also was the work of the deacons. These things occupy a great part of Christian work. This category of things is what everyone in the church must properly learn before God.

HELPING IN HOUSEHOLD CHORES

Brothers and sisters, at this point I think I can make a suggestion. Please pay close attention to this. There are many brothers and sisters who have some spare time. There are also many sisters at home who have no time whatever. They have to cook, and they have to take care of their children. Why would the brothers in the service of the Levites not take responsibility in this matter by actually arranging for someone to go to their home to help them? The responsible ones can tell them that there are two sisters among us who can help them do the laundry two hours every week. This is also the work of the Levites. At the time of the apostles, the widows of the Hellenists were not adequately being cared for, and there were murmurings. Such was the church. Although this was not something spiritual, but rather a practical affair, it still needed to be done.

TWELVE ITEMS OF PRACTICAL AFFAIRS

There are many things that we can consider before the Lord: (1) the cleaning work; (2) the arranging of the hall and the work of ushering; (3) the need for a group of brothers and sisters to take care of the breaking of bread and the baptisms. Some need to be responsible for the bread and the cup for the bread-breaking meeting. We also need some who are trained to take care of the matters related to baptisms, such as helping those who are being baptized go down and come up out of the water, change their clothes, etc. (4) Giving to the poor among the unbelievers. When unbelievers are involved in disasters of floods or fire, the church should take care of them. (5) Caring for those who are poor among us; (6) the receiving and sending of brothers; (7) the bookkeeping; (8) the kitchen service; (9) the service office; (10) the transportation service. In places where cars or vans are available, some need to oversee their use. (11) The clerical work, which includes handling the incoming and outgoing mail; and (12) helping the poor brothers and sisters do their household chores, including laundry, sewing, mending, etc.

I also expect that every brother and sister will bear the

burden in practical affairs. Never let a situation exist where some have things to do and others are doing nothing. The service of the church is always for everyone. If there are some brothers and sisters in our midst who have time, it would be good for them to help other brothers and sisters in their housework. Every week they could go to another brother's or sister's house to help for an hour or two, doing some miscellaneous things for them. Especially, it would be good for those sisters who are housewives with wealth and good standing to go to some brother's or sister's house to do some washing and mending. They should not just have people working for them, while they themselves do nothing. It befits them as Christians to go to the homes of poor brothers and sisters and do things with their own hands.

THE PRINCIPLE OF EVERYONE SERVING

I have said enough concerning the practical affairs. You have to be clear before God about this principle that all the brothers and sisters must have spiritual service as well as practical service. It does not matter how much everyone can do. I expect that everyone will work and do his best. If this matter can be properly arranged, the church will be able to progress step by step. Brothers, I say again that you must realize that the responsibility upon you is very great and that the things in your hands will keep you very busy. You have to work to such an extent that you bring all the brothers to the same condition that you are in. When all the brothers come and serve together, the church in that locality will have a foundation. When others see this, they will know the church is in our midst. Everyone works, everyone shares in the practical affairs, and everyone participates in the spiritual things.

CAUSING ALL THE ONE-TALENTED ONES
TO DO BUSINESS

I would like to speak to the responsible brothers. You have a natural habit of using only the two-talented ones. The history of the church has always been like this. The five-talented ones can advance by themselves; there is no need to take care of them. But as for the one-talented ones, it is really hard to help them. A word or two to them and they bury their talent again. The two-talented ones are the most available ones. They have some ability, they can do things well, and they do not bury their talents. But if you can use only the two-talented ones and cannot use the one-talented ones in every place, you have failed completely. I have said this in Foochow, I have said this in Shanghai, and I will say it again today. What is the church? The church is all the one-talented ones coming forth to partake of the church service on the practical side and on the spiritual side. You cannot shake your head and say, "This one is useless, and that one is useless." If you say that this one is useless and that one is useless, the church is finished and you fail completely. If you think someone is useless, he will really be useless. You can tell him that according to himself he is indeed useless, but the Lord has given him one talent, and He wants all the one-talented ones to go out and do business. The Lord can use them. If you cannot use the one-talented ones, it proves that before the Lord you cannot be a leader. You have to use all those brothers and sisters who are "useless." This is the job of the brothers who are workers. They must not only use the useful brothers and sisters but also make the useless brothers and sisters useful.

The basic principle is that the Lord has never given less than one talent to anyone. In the Lord's house there is not one servant without a gift; everyone has at least one talent and cannot have less than one talent. No one can excuse himself by saying that the Lord has not given him a talent. I would like you to realize that all of God's children are servants before Him. If they are children, they are servants. In other words, if they are members, they have a gift; if they are members, they are ministers. If we think that there is someone whom the Lord cannot use, we do not know the grace of God at all. We must know the grace of God so thoroughly that when God calls someone His servant, we would never stand up to say that he is not. Today if you did the choosing, perhaps you would pick only three or four persons from the whole church. But God says that all are servants. Since God says this, we must let them serve.

Brothers and sisters, from now on whether or not we have a way in our work and whether or not the way will succeed depend upon what we can say about our work before the Lord. Are there only some who are working? Are only some specially gifted ones doing the work? Or do all the Lord's servants participate in the service, and is the whole church serving? This is the entire problem. If this problem cannot be solved, we have nothing.

THE BODY OF CHRIST BEING LIVING

The Body of Christ is not a doctrine; it is something living. We all must learn this one thing: Only when every member functions is there the Body of Christ. Only when every member functions is that the church.

Our problem today is that we have inherited the priestly system of Roman Catholicism and the pastoral system of Protestantism. If we are careless at the present time, there will also appear a certain kind of mediatorial system among us. We will be the only ones who take care of the matters in God's service. Merely preaching the Body of Christ is useless; we must let it work and show forth its functions. Since it is the Body of Christ, we need not fear that it will lack the functions. Since it is the Body of Christ, we can place our faith in it. The Lord wants every member in every locality to rise up and serve.

GOD HAVING GONE AHEAD OF US

If I am right, according to my discernment it is possible that the time has come. The letters I have received from different places and the news I have heard from every place indicate that today in every place all the saints are ready to come forth to serve. God has gone ahead of us; we must follow Him.

It is not my desire that even one brother from among us would go out and fail to lead the brothers and sisters to serve but would replace them instead. I hope that when you go to a certain place, you will lead eight or ten to serve at the beginning and then after a certain time they will lead sixty, eighty, or a hundred to serve. Then on your next visit you may see one or two thousand people serving. This is proper. If you must use the five-talented ones to suppress the two-talented ones and the two-talented ones to suppress the one-talented ones, you are not the Lord's servant. If you must use the five-talented ones to replace the two-talented ones and the two-talented ones to replace the one-talented ones, you are not the Lord's servant. You must cause all the five-talented ones to rise up and serve and all the two-talented ones to rise up and serve, and you must also cause all the one-talented ones to rise up and serve. You must also cause those whom you think are not useful to rise up and serve. Thus, the glorious church will appear.

In Foochow I would rather see all the simple villagers serving than three or five outstanding ones preaching. I do not admire the outstanding ones. I like the one-talented ones.

In His graciousness the Lord could give us more Pauls and Peters, but He has not done so. The whole world is full of one-talented brothers and sisters. What shall we do with these people? Where are we going to put them?

PHILADELPHIA MUST APPEAR

In this training here on the mountain, if God really deals with our self and with our work to the extent that we go out to provide a way for all the one-talented ones to serve, for the first time the church will begin to see what brotherly love is and Philadelphia will appear.

Today the church needs not only oversight but also brotherly love. I believe in authority, and I also believe in brotherly love. Without authority the church cannot go on. "And have kept My word"—this is authority. "And have not denied My name"—this is authority. Philadelphia had these two kinds of authority. But Philadelphia herself is brotherly love. All the brothers come forth and serve in love. When such a day comes, we will begin to know what the church is. Otherwise, if the present condition continues, we will still be hanging on to the tail of Roman Catholicism and Protestantism; we will not know what the brothers of Philadelphia are and what the authority of the church is.

TWO WAYS—GIFT AND AUTHORITY

Today I think that two ways are clearly set before us. If the Lord can really break through in our midst, the way we have taken for the past ten, twenty, or thirty years will be completely reversed. Our view cannot be the same as before; it has to be broken and crushed.

Not Leaving Anyone Out

First, you should not use a brother just because he is useful and leave him out if he is not useful. In the church no member should be left out. This is not the way taken by the Lord. Today, if the Lord is going to recover His testimony, He must make all the one-talented ones rise up. All who belong to the Lord are the members of the Body. Everyone must rise up and be in his function. If this is the case, you will see the church. While you are here on the mountain, consider every place. You almost have to say, "Where is the church? Where is Christ?" It seems that neither the church nor the Lord is there. When you go out, never despise the one-talented ones, never replace them, and never suppress them. You have to trust them from your heart. You have to cause them to work. If God has the assurance to call them to be servants, you too should have the assurance to call them to be servants.

Authority Dealing with the Flesh

Second, in the church we are not afraid of fleshly activities. Two lines are to be established in the church—one is authority and the other is gift. All the one-talented ones must come forth to serve, work, and bear fruit. You may ask, "If the one-talented ones come forth with their flesh, what shall we do?" Let me say that the flesh must be dealt with, and the way to deal with it is by using the authority which represents God.

Gift and authority are two entirely distinct things; gift is gift, and authority is authority. The one-talented ones must use their gift, and with those who are fleshly, you must use authority. If a brother brings in the flesh while he is working, you must tell him, "Brother, that will not do. You cannot bring that in." Tell him, "This attitude is wrong. We do not allow you to have this attitude." When you speak with him in this way, he will probably go home the next day and not do anything anymore. Then you will have to look him up and say, "No, you still should do the work." The flesh may come in again, but you still must let him do the work. You must say to him again, "You must do this, but we will not allow you to do that." Always use authority to deal with him.

This is the greatest test. Once the Lord uses the one-talented ones, their flesh will immediately be brought in. The flesh and the one talent are joined together. We must refuse the flesh, but we have to use that one talent. Today's situation is that we bury the flesh, they bury the one talent, and the church has nothing. This cannot be! We have to use authority to deal with the flesh, but we also have to ask them to bring forth their talent. Perhaps they will say, "If I work, it will not do, and if I do not work, it will not do either. So what shall I do?" You must say to them, "Indeed, if you work, it is wrong because you bring in the flesh; but if you do not work, it is also wrong because you bury the talent. The one talent must come in, but not the flesh."

In the church if the authority can be maintained and the functions of all the members brought in, you will see a glorious church on the earth, and the way of recovery will be easy. I do not know how many more days the Lord has set before us. I believe our way will be clearer and clearer. We need to use all our thought and all our strength so that all the brothers and sisters may rise up and serve. When that time comes, the church will be manifested and the Lord will return. May the Lord be merciful and gracious to us so that we may do the best.

CHAPTER SIX

THE WAY FOR THE WORK HEREAFTER

(A talk given to the co-workers as trainees on Mount Kuling, August 19, 1948, and published in *The Ministers,* dated November 1, 1948.)

Our former pathway in the Lord's work has caused us to encounter some practical difficulties. This year we have spent considerable time to solve our problem through the two meetings in Foochow and Shanghai. Today we will come back again to this matter.

THE PROBLEM OF THE PAST

While we saw the light concerning the church quite clearly in the past, we did not see the light concerning the work so well. *The Normal Christian Church Life,* which was published following a co-workers' conference in Hankow, shows that our vision was clear about the matter of the church. We saw that the churches are local, a matter which is much clearer today than throughout the history of the church. By reading many books, we certainly can realize that the local character of the church has never been as clear as it is today. In relation to the work, however, we have always felt that we lacked the same clarity. This was because Jerusalem seemed to be superfluous when viewed from the perspective of Antioch. When we were in Hankow, we surveyed the entire book of Acts, but we were not able to take Jerusalem into account. Starting from chapter thirteen, the book of Acts lined up with our work, and our work lined up with the book of Acts. However, we did not know how to apply the events that occurred before Acts 13. At that time we did not have sufficient light.

Due to the trials and difficulties we have encountered during these several years, we now see the usefulness of the first ten or more chapters of Acts. We have discovered the usefulness of these chapters. Please pardon me for speaking in this way, but this is the fact. We have to acknowledge that through the meetings in Foochow and Shanghai the first twelve chapters of Acts have become clearer to us than ever before. Just as the local churches after Acts 13 have never been seen with such clarity as in the time at Hankow, the work has never been seen with such clarity as it is today. The difficulties in the past are in the past; today the situation is different.

THE WORK BEING REGIONAL

One of several matters that we discovered relates to regions. While churches are local, the work is regional. This, I feel, is very clearly revealed in the Scriptures. We did not see this five or ten years ago because we just did not see it; we could not help it. Now, however, we have definitely seen it, and it can be stated in just two phrases: The churches are local, and the work is regional. In other words, the church is local, but the work is regional, being composed of many localities combined together to form a region.

In the book of Acts it can be clearly seen that the twelve apostles had a definite region for their work. Peter, John, and their group worked in one region, while Paul, Silas, Timothy, and Barnabas worked in another region. In the first chapter of Philippians, we can see many different regions. In 2 Corinthians 10:13-14, we find these words: "But we will not boast beyond our measure but according to the measure of the rule which the God of measure has apportioned to us, to reach even as far as you. For we are not extending ourselves beyond our bounds." Here we are clearly shown something related to a region, a measure that God apportioned to the apostles. God drew a circle for them, and within that circle there was an area of work for them. Therefore, the work is related to the matter of region.

The churches, however, are not related to a region. No church should exercise control over other localities, because the churches are local.

In the past we made a great mistake in confusing the sphere of the work with the locality of the church. Now we clearly see that the work includes a number of localities within a certain area called a region. Just as Peter and John were in the region around Jerusalem, Paul and Timothy were in another region around Antioch. Although they maintained contact and fellowship with each other, their respective regions were not the same.

Today we cannot speak too much, but it is more than clear that the work is regional and the churches are local.

REGIONS HAVING CENTERS

The second matter involves a center in each region. The churches do not have a center. The church in Jerusalem had no control over the churches in Samaria. Those who study the Bible know that churches are local and that a church in one locality cannot exercise control over a church in another locality. Moreover, the church in one locality cannot control the churches in many localities. The highest place a church can appeal to is its own locality; there is no district council or headquarters for the church. However, this is not so with the work, because the work has a center. In the book of Acts we can say that Jerusalem was a center in one region, while Antioch was a center in another region.

The Special Characteristic of Jerusalem

If we did not realize that the work has a center, Jerusalem would become a problem rather than a help. Even though the Bible reveals that churches are local, Jerusalem seems to be somewhat special, and even though the Bible reveals that the churches are local, Antioch seems to be special. Consequently, Antioch can become a problem rather than a help to us also. Both Jerusalem and Antioch can present problems rather than help to us.

Today, we see clearly that the church in Antioch is one thing, while Antioch as a center for the work is another. When speaking of the churches, Jerusalem stands equal with Antioch and also with the churches in Samaria. When speaking of the work, however, Jerusalem is the center of the work. God's command was that there would be witnesses in Jerusalem and in all Judea and Samaria and unto the uttermost parts of the earth. Jerusalem was a center of the work.

In Acts 13, there was another beginning in Antioch, and Antioch became another center of the work. The Holy Spirit started something there. The Holy Spirit made one start in Jerusalem, and the Holy Spirit made another start in Antioch in Acts 13. In both places the Holy Spirit started the work. From Antioch, some went forth to other places to do a work. When churches came into being, elders were appointed to be responsible for the oversight of the churches. But it seems that Antioch was responsible for them, because the workers lived in Antioch.

Peter Also Being an Elder

Here we see the preciousness of Jerusalem. In reading the Scriptures we also see the preciousness of Peter being an elder in Jerusalem. In the past we only paid attention to Peter as an apostle rather than to Peter as an elder. He was in a double position. In relation to the locality of Jerusalem, Peter was an elder, James was an elder, and John was an elder. In relation to the work, however, they were all apostles. Therefore, when they wrote letters to the church in Antioch, they signed as apostles and elders. Otherwise, it would have been impossible for the elders in Jerusalem to write and give orders to the church in Antioch, because the church in Antioch had elders as well. As elders, they told the church in Antioch what decisions they had made for the church in Jerusalem; as apostles, they also made the same decisions for the work.

Today this matter is very clear among us. With us this problem has been entirely solved; it is behind us. Not only is it behind us, but this very teaching has been gloriously brought forth. Now we see that God's work is carried out by a region. For His work God wants to establish a locality as a center. All of the workers should be centralized in that locality, sometimes going out and sometimes coming back. The elders are responsible for a local church, but if a locality is also a center for the work, then the workers should also be elders to share in the responsibility of church affairs there, in addition to just the elders.

The Scriptures do not offer one example of sending workers to reside in a locality. Such a practice is not found in the

Bible. The only exception to this is when a worker migrates to a locality and becomes an elder there. An elder may choose to reside in Jerusalem or he may move to another city to be an elder in that city. He can take up responsibility in the respective cities where he resides. However, if a person wants to be a worker, he should move to Jerusalem.

The church has accused Peter for the past two thousand years, but we have to say that Peter was not wrong. The church has accused Peter during the past two thousand years of not leaving Jerusalem, but it was right for Peter to remain in Jerusalem; it was not wrong. Some have said that Peter should have left Jerusalem, but I do not believe this! Who can say that the Lord wanted Peter and John to leave Jerusalem? Some have said that Peter and John brought persecutions to the church in Jerusalem because they did not leave. This, however, has no scriptural ground. If the Lord desired that Peter and John leave Jerusalem, He could have caused persecution to fall upon Peter and John, not upon the church. It is not right for me to be wrong and others suffer for it. If the Lord caused others to suffer, then surely I am not wrong. If it was wrong for Peter and John to remain in Jerusalem, God should have rebuked Peter and John; He should not have brought persecution to the church in Jerusalem.

However, the Lord said that the world would hate us because we are not of the world, and that if the world persecuted Him, it would also persecute us (John 15:19-20). When we follow the Lord, the world hates us because we are not of the world. Persecution does not occur because we fail to leave our home. If this were the case, all Christians who left their homes would be spared from persecution. Persecution is experienced equally by Christians who stay at home and those who leave their homes.

Going Out and Coming Back

You will remember that Peter went out to Caesarea and returned to Jerusalem. Then Peter went to Samaria (because the work of God was in Samaria) and then returned to Jerusalem. Jerusalem was the center, whereas Samaria was a city in that region of work. The co-workers gathered in Jerusalem. They went out and came back, came back and went out.

Having a worker rule over a church in a locality is a Protestant thought; it is not the thought of the Scriptures. Only God can make the decision as to which locality should be taken as the center for the work. Only God knows how and where to start; only the Holy Spirit knows how to initiate the work. Man's decision is of no use. We cannot decide which locality is "Jerusalem" through our own discussion, because God wants to do that Himself. This matter is in the hands of the Holy Spirit. Only the Jerusalem appointed by the Holy Spirit is Jerusalem.

In the first part of Acts, we see Peter going out and coming back to Jerusalem. Later, we see Paul going out and coming back to Antioch. They never remained in a locality but always came back. We must see that the work has an area as well as a center.

Whether we call it a region, an area, or a center, these are but terms. We need to emphasize the essential thing behind the terms. In the work in Jerusalem there was something essential. It matters not whether we call it an area, a center, or a region. The same is true with Antioch. Since the Lord measures a portion to a work, it is right to call it the measure of the work. One group of workers dwells in one area, region, or center, while another group of workers dwells in another.

Elders are not assigned to certain places from other places. In the case of Peter, he was not simply an apostle, and he was not simply an elder. He was both an apostle and an elder. Therefore, brothers, when you, as a co-worker, reside in a locality, you are there as both an apostle and an elder. Taking this path in such a way is correct. It is right that some of our brothers go out to help, but they must come back. It is not right for them to stay and not return. Either they go out and travel a large circuit and then return like Paul, or they go out and immediately return like Peter—both are right. Coming back is a must. If men blame Peter for not going out, they have to blame Paul for returning as well. Peter returned to Jerusalem, and Paul to Antioch. This is God's Word; nothing can be clearer than His Word.

THE APOSTLES' PREACHING OF THE GOSPEL AND THE PREACHING BY THE WAY OF MIGRATION

Now we will see the third matter, that is, how the work of God is carried forward and how the gospel is preached. Here we have two ways. As the work of Jerusalem is different from that of Antioch, so we have two different ways of preaching the gospel and two different ways of establishing churches.

The Way of Antioch—the Apostles Going Out

First, it can be done according to Antioch's way. Paul and Barnabas, Paul and Timothy, or Paul and Silas went to one place after another to preach the gospel and then returned to Antioch. It was the apostles who went out to preach the gospel and the apostles who went out to establish churches. This is one way.

The Way of Jerusalem—Going Out by Migration

The second way is Jerusalem's way. In this way all the believers migrated. They preached the gospel in every place. This migration resulted in the gospel spreading everywhere (Acts 8:4). Whether a migration is done peacefully or as a result of persecution, a migration is still a migration. The way of Jerusalem is to migrate. The only thing special was that they went out because of persecution.

I think that the Lord has left very clear footprints here. We should never think that the first half of Acts is of little significance. Acts, like Genesis, is a record of God's way. When we see how God worked at the beginning, we can do the same today.

The Measure of Increase Being in Proportion to the Number Going Out

God used persecution to force the saints to migrate. They could not stay; they were compelled to leave. At that time thousands of people were constantly going out. But Paul still found thousands of believers in the church upon his return to Jerusalem. When he came back to Jerusalem and went to see James and all the elders, he was told of many thousands of Jews there who had believed (Acts 21:20). Wheat that is harvested this year will grow again next year. We must leave the ground we have occupied in order to allow others to become Christians. We should not remain stationary all the time. The number of Christians going out is indicative of increase in the same proportion. Staying all the time in one place will not cause our numbers to increase. The disciples in Jerusalem continued to go out to preach the gospel, yet the Bible says that there were thousands of Jewish believers when Paul returned to Jerusalem. God's way is to send people out group by group like scattered seeds.

Before God we need to see clearly these three principles before we can engage in so-called missionary work.

The Need to Preach the Gospel

When I was in London, I once told Mr. Austin-Sparks that our work in China is different from their work—we must take care of the gospel first. Since there are so many Christians in all parts of London, it seems as if the whole country is Christian. But in China, we must work according to the primitive pattern of first preaching the gospel. It seems that the work our brother is doing in London is only a work of ministry. As for us, we must preach the gospel.

Not Being Slack

Therefore, brothers, we must never be slack regarding these three points. During the many years of the Sino-Japanese War, we encountered numerous difficulties. Through these difficulties we learned these things. For many of us, at least half of our time is gone. The remaining half must be spent in taking a straight course. We should never walk as in the past. I believe (this is my personal feeling) that this light is sufficiently clear. For two thousand years the church has tried to make Jerusalem fit into the whole picture, but it has never been made to fit correctly. Today we are able to make it fit correctly and even clearly. This matter is now as clear as the truth we saw in Hankow concerning the locality of the church.

To us, it is clear that the churches are local, and it is clear that the work is regional. For this reason our work needs to be on the right track. If we still think that a worker should handle a locality, we will reach an impasse. Unless this matter is dealt with, the work can never go on. The old way will not work. For example, if the old way were right, then we would not have enough co-workers to take care of the more than one hundred meetings in the P'ing Yang region, even if we sent them all. We would not have enough co-workers for the Wenchow region. We would need the sisters to be pastors. Following this way, we would never be able to meet the needs.

Maintaining the Testimony at the Center

We must see that the work has its region and its center. All matters pertaining to the localities can be placed in the hands of the local churches. The workers always go out to work. After a short while they return to Jerusalem. Then they move out again and return again to Jerusalem. For this reason, it is good to maintain a strong testimony in Jerusalem. It is an easy task for the twelve apostles to maintain the ministry of the word in Jerusalem, but it would be too difficult for them to maintain this ministry throughout Samaria and all Judea.

Therefore, before God we need to have much prayer and clear light concerning which locality can be used as the center for the work in a region. It has to be a place where a group of co-workers, both brothers and sisters, may dwell together and establish a center. It should also be the place where they serve as members of the local church to maintain the local testimony. By going out and coming back, the ministry of the word in that locality is properly maintained.

Shanghai Being a Center

For the provinces of Kiangsu and Chekiang, the center of the work along the Nanking-Shanghai and Shanghai-Hangchow railways lines is in Shanghai. Therefore, Shanghai must maintain a strong testimony, and Shanghai needs workers to maintain the work. The responsibility of the rest of the localities in this region should be left to the brothers of their own locality. At the same time the brothers in Shanghai should migrate to other places. After a period of time, the brothers in Shanghai should move out group by group. This is a very important matter. Going out to preach the gospel is in the hand of the brothers and sisters; we are not sending people out to be pastors, but just to be emigrants. Please remember that the principle of Jerusalem is migration. This was the method for preaching the gospel in the early churches. One can say that they went out because of persecution. But then where do we find children of God who do not suffer persecution? Hence, we must bear in mind that the path is clearly laid before us.

Foochow Also Being a Center

This is how I see this matter today. I may illustrate it in this way: If the province of Fukien and the island of Taiwan are one region for the work, we believe that Foochow may be taken as a center. Of course, the brothers must support and maintain such a center by going out and coming back. When we bring people to salvation, we should admonish them that they too must go out by the Lord's grace. We should encourage twenty people to move to Nan-Ping, thirty to Putien, thirty to Amoy, thirty to Taipei, and thirty also to Tainan. When they move out, the gospel will go out with them. The gospel will simply follow them. If we are expecting a considerable number of evangelists to be raised up within a certain number of years, not only will the expense be high, but the number of people going out will be limited. Eventually, we will not see much result. Remember that the whole church must go forth to preach the gospel. It is right for group after group to go out.

In Foochow there are apostles and elders. Sometimes two or three of them may go to a locality to visit and then return. Two or three more may go to another locality and also return.

I am not saying that all the gospel work must be left in their hands from now on. Perhaps one or two brothers and sisters need to visit from village to village. But the gospel will go out only when these two ways of carrying the gospel are taken at the same time.

The Ministry of the Word and the Sending Out

We now can see that the work at the center becomes very important. There we not only need to maintain the ministry of the Word, but we also need to send people out for the work. Regardless of whether they are peddlers, rickshaw coolies or domestic servants, they all must be sent out to preach the gospel.

For this reason, we need to give all the brothers and sisters a proper training so that they will be brought to the point where they are ready to be sent out. Fifty will be sent to one place and thirty to another place where they will be able to help the local churches without becoming a burden to them. If the many who are sent forth become a problem and the local churches cannot deal with them, what good is this? Therefore, the brothers and sisters need to be properly trained in order to be prepared to go out as missionaries group by group.

The co-workers must see that the work has to be centralized, not scattered. The locality which is the center first must be set up in good order before the saints can be trained and sent out.

During the past few years we have encountered many sufferings and difficulties. We have learned some lessons. May we not treat these lessons lightly. We need to learn from these things.

THE NEED TO RECEIVE BASIC TRAINING

Now we come to the fourth point, that is, the need for all the brothers and sisters to receive the same training.

The New Believers' Training Meeting

We need to offer the new believers a special kind of meeting. In Shanghai and Foochow we have already offered this training to the new believing brothers and sisters. This meeting is the same every year. We do not want to move on to something new. Of course, we do not want these training lessons to be recited like the Lord's prayer to some people. If the speakers are living, there will be life. These instructional lessons are given in sequence from the beginning of each year to the end. After fifty-two weeks, the cycle is repeated again. When each brother goes out, he will at least have received all the basic instructions. In this way, we will eliminate some of the problems.

If some come into our midst, regardless of which week they join, they will finish the whole training in one year. After fifty-two weeks, the cycle will repeat itself again. If they come in at the tenth week of the first year, they will complete the cycle of training and teaching when they approach the ninth week of the following year. Everyone should get the same instructions and then be ready to be sent out.

Sent Out to Preach the Gospel

Advise them that when they migrate to a place they should try their best to save souls in the locality where they live. Thus, we should first bring men to salvation in the locality which is the center. These people should be edified and sent out to other places. They should be given the opportunity to go out to preach the gospel.

In this way the whole church will preach the gospel, not just the evangelists. If only the evangelists do the preaching, they can never complete the preaching of the gospel throughout China in their lifetime. Today the population in China is 450 million, but not more than one million are Christians. If these one million Christians are in our hand and everyone is sent out, we can evangelize China. We need to help them receive the same kind of training and then send them out. Then we will see the church preaching the gospel everywhere.

They go out to preach the gospel because they are sent out, not because they are persecuted. Perhaps they will meet persecution, but the main thing is that they must go out.

Some arrangement is necessary, and the leading brothers must make these arrangements. Some localities are strategic geographically, and we must take them. Perhaps we first should send three or five men there to take up some kind of employment. Then we might send a few more to take up other employment. When people are brought to salvation through them, the co-workers can then go there to raise up a meeting. In order to go on, we need a change from the present situation. This is the way to go on in the work.

The Church Being Fruitful
When It Preaches the Gospel

Today all the brothers and sisters acknowledge that when the church preaches the gospel there is always more fruit. Only the work of the church can become more fruitful. Recently, a group of brothers went to Kutien to preach the gospel, and a total of more than fifty were saved and baptized. Brother Chen returned and said that when he left he did not know what the result of the church's preaching of the gospel would be. But after his trip to Kutien, he had no more doubts: When the church preached the gospel, men were saved. Without advertisement, one person simply took hold of one or two other persons. In a short time more than fifty were saved.

In the past Nan-Ping had only a few saints in the meetings. After the brothers went there recently, more than twenty people were baptized. These people heard the gospel during the great fire in Nan-Ping, when only one fourth of the city was spared. About ten homes of our brothers were also burned. Brother Huang's store was burned too. But when the whole church preached the gospel, a number of people were saved. Our brothers wrote and said that since they discovered this way, they would give their lives for it and not turn in any other direction.

While the church is preaching the gospel, the Lord is working. We did not have to use any advertisement or apply any human methods. The brothers simply went out, each one bringing in another, and the people came. It matters little if the message is somewhat weak. As long as the church is preaching the gospel, scores upon scores of people will be baptized. In the future this work will be passed on to the local brothers; they will do the work themselves.

Kuling Will Furnish Help

What should we do here in Kuling Mountain? The local churches should send promising ones here to be given one or two months of spiritual help. Then they will be sent back to their localities to bear some responsibility. The co-workers should always bear the responsibility of the work in the center, but they also should go out and return again and again. If we do this, the work will have a way to go on.

The Need for Coordination

For this reason, during the conferences in both Shanghai and Foochow, we paid much attention to the matter of coordination. Nothing will work without coordination. In the past, we were all going our own way, but without coordination nothing can be done properly. No one should act independently; everyone must give himself to be properly coordinated.

I believe that the gospel will spread quickly. Moreover, I believe that it will be easy for us to take over the whole of China. For instance, if the brothers in Foochow are faithful, it will be very easy for them to take over Fukien province and the island of Taiwan. If the brothers in other localities are also faithful and learn to take this way, they will also be able to take over their places.

Today we have found the way. Now it is altogether a matter of the person. The way cannot be clearer. If we do not see the principle of Jerusalem, we will feel that there is something in the Word of God which does not fit; it seems as if there is some problem. Today we have to declare that the whole book of Acts fits in very well; there is no problem. Furthermore, each time I read the book of Acts now, I marvel at the way Peter conducted himself in the first part. I think Peter has been unjustly accused for two thousand years. Peter's going out and coming back to Jerusalem was altogether correct. Undoubtedly, there are centers for God's work.

The Ministry of the Word
No Longer Being a Problem

If we take this way, the matter of the ministry of the word will no longer be a problem. All we have to do is maintain such a ministry in one central locality. The other localities need to be led to take care of themselves. There will be no problem with the ministry of the word if the local ones are the ones that are taking care of the matter themselves. It is for this cause that we in Kuling are preparing a place for training. In the future we will bring all the good, prospective ones from all the churches here to receive some training. Then we will send them back. Thus, I will do my work and you will do your work, each one attending to his own work. I believe that we can soon get through this way and strong testimonies can be built up continuously in many localities.

The Foundation of the Work

The foundation of all the work today is here. If this becomes confused, everything will be confused, and we will revert back to the situation before our gathering in Hankow. In Hankow we only saw the matter of the church; at that time we did not see the matter of the work. Now the way of the work is before us. If we have the right people and the mercy of the Lord is with us, within a few years the gospel will be spread all over China. I believe this is a great eventuality—to preach the gospel to all of China. Unless we take this way, the situation will remain the same for fifty years.

I acknowledge that much of God's blessing has been in our midst. In the past I have said that God always saves people. As a matter of fact, God has saved quite a number of people in our midst. However, I always feel that this is not enough; we still have not saved enough people. Recently, we all gave ourselves to study the Bible again. I myself have read God's Word once or twice again. I find God's Word becoming so very clear. In the past we only saw the way of the church. We did not see the way of the work. When the way of the work is not proper, the way of the church is not proper either. We thank God for His mercy upon us that today He has opened our eyes to see this way after so many years. The brothers in a locality must always bear their responsibilities. They must practice coordination, and they must migrate to other places group by group to preach the gospel.

This is a very simple matter. Jerusalem had great success in this matter. Before God, Jerusalem represents the church. The heavenly Jerusalem represents the church, and the earthly Jerusalem also represents the church. Peter was always working there, and as a result, many people went out to preach the gospel. Never do we see the gospel coming to an end when the people left. The gospel will go on continually. This is exceedingly glorious.

TODAY'S REQUIREMENT— BEING FAITHFUL IN COORDINATION

Therefore, today there is a requirement not only for the co-workers to be coordinated but for the leading ones to be coordinated as well. None of us can choose freely. In this way the church will preach the gospel. Every person, no matter where he goes, must go for the gospel. Their mouth must be for the preaching of the gospel. We need to go out as the Body. I believe that the Lord will have His way today.

If we are not trustworthy and faithful, the Lord will choose others to take this way. I believe that it is possible for Him to do this, but it would take at least another twenty years. Do not say that the Lord will not lay us aside. The Lord can easily lay us aside, but it would waste another twenty years. We expect to save twenty years for the Lord. May the Lord have mercy on us so that we may catch up. Let us give our all for this. After passing through very burdensome and difficult experiences, He has shown us this way. May we not forsake it.

A message given by Watchman Nee and recorded by Brother Chou on the morning of August 19, 1948.